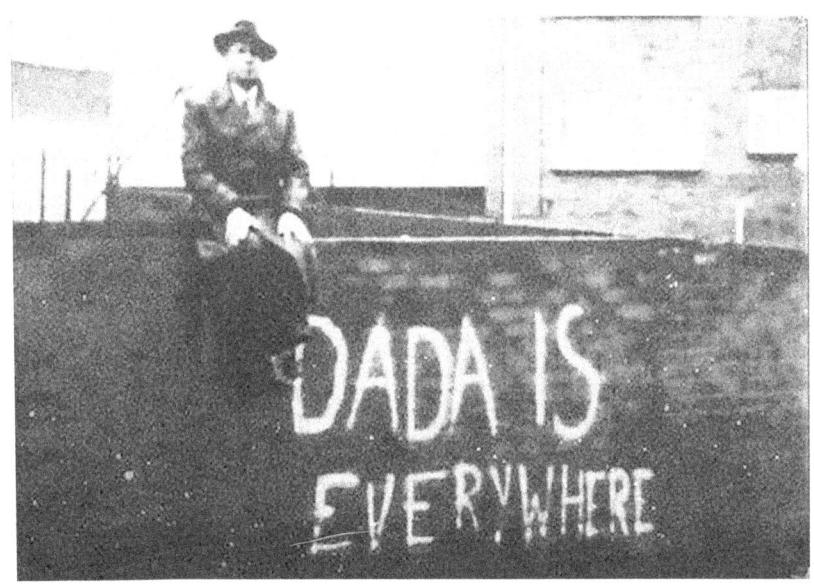

THE LIFE AND WORK OF
GEORGE MELLY

by Chris Wade

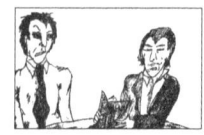

THE LIFE AND WORK OF GEORGE MELLY
by Chris Wade

Wisdom Twins Books, 2018
wisdomtwinsbooks.weebly.com

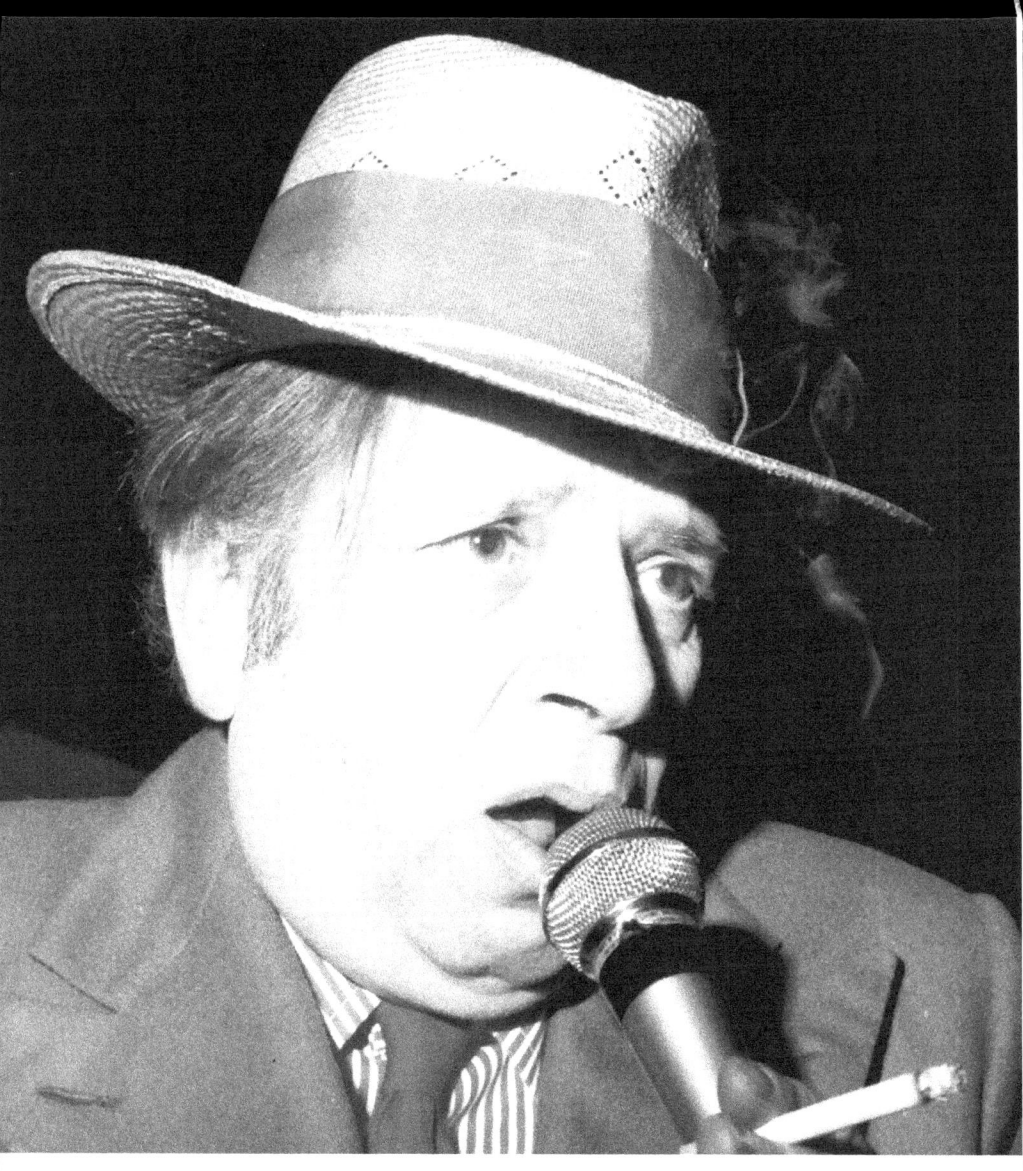

THE LIFE AND WORK OF
GEORGE MELLY

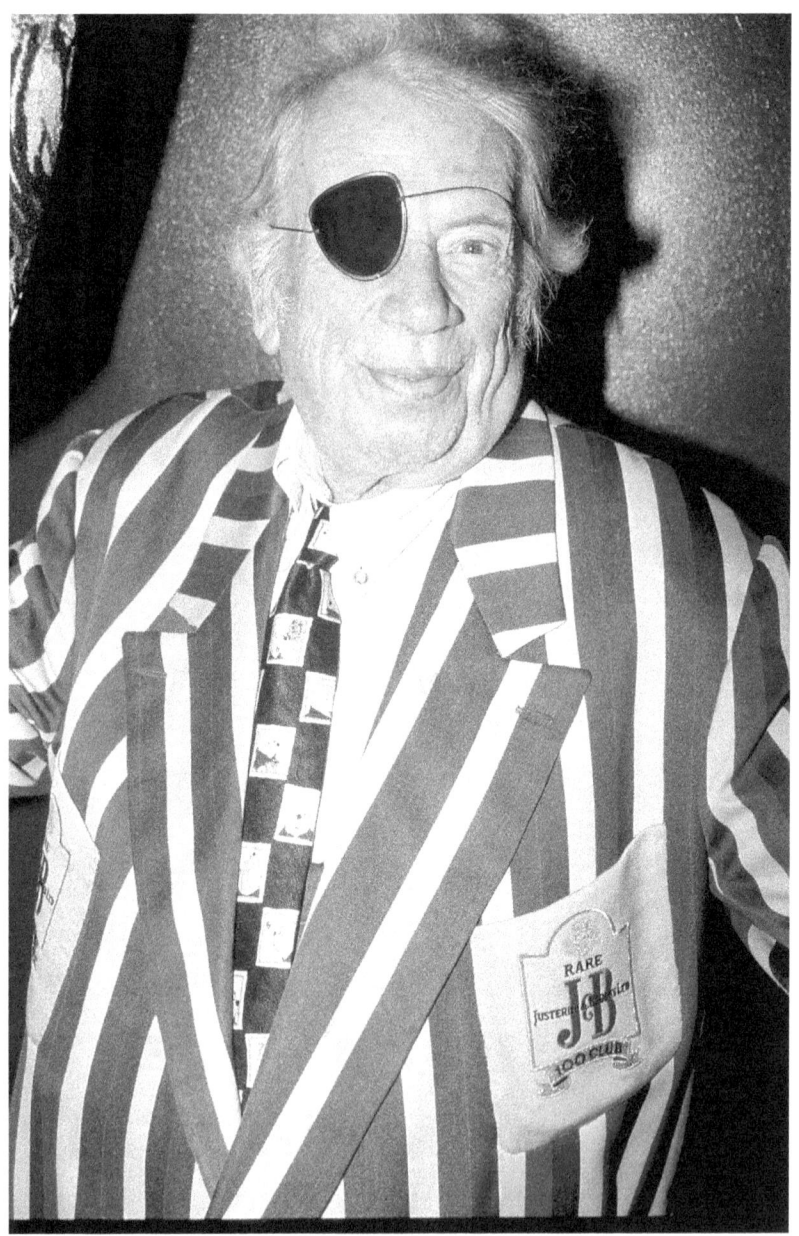

4

CONTENTS

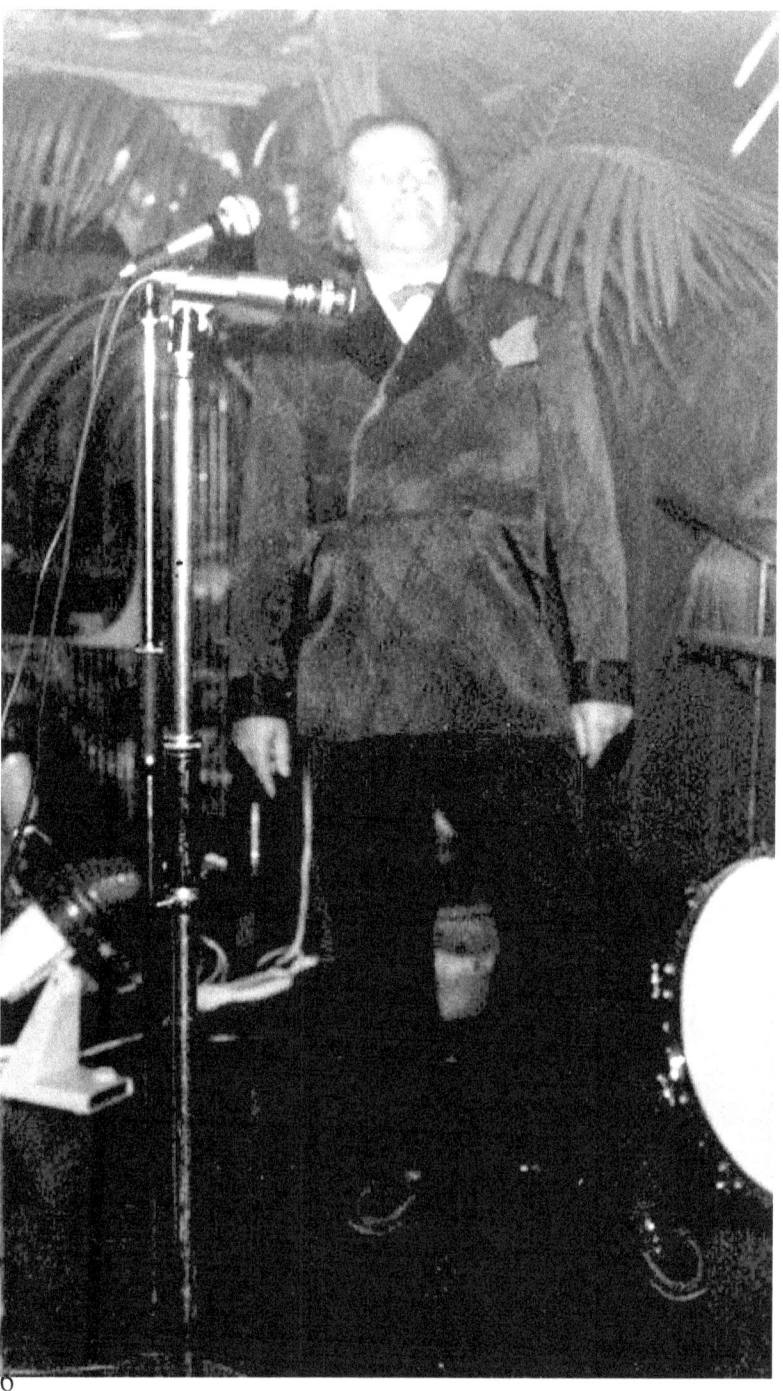

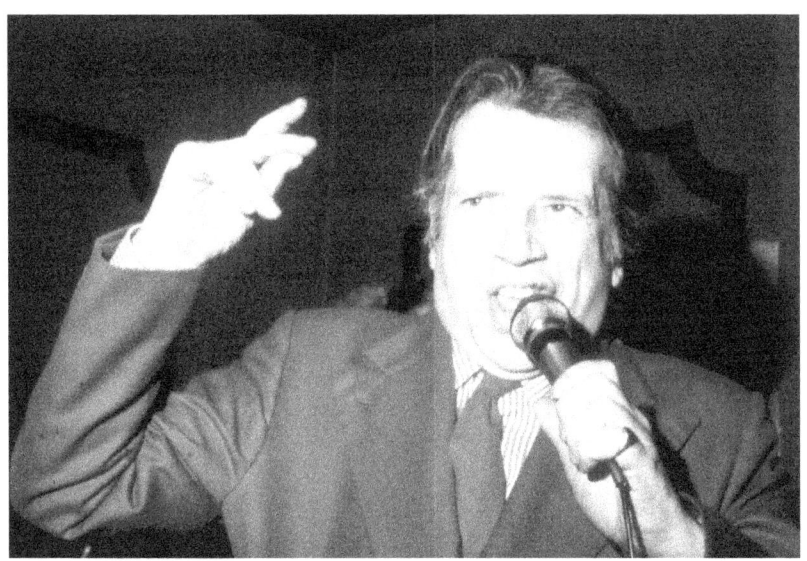

INTRODUCTION

"With an insatiable appetite for life and razor sharp wit, I defy anyone
to take a flick through one of the autobiographical works of jazz
man, critic and raconteur George Melly and not come away
convinced that this larger than life character invented rebellion..."

- Martin Quirk, Sabotage Times

This book is dedicated to the extraordinary life and work of George
Melly, the late jazz singer, eccentric, film critic, writer, raver,
raconteur, Surrealist, art lover, chronicler of bawdy memoirs and all
round cultural legend. Though it applies, legend might be the wrong
choice of word. Perhaps, as George's friend Digby Fairweather
dubbed him in an email to me, Melly would have preferred the term
icon. Melly noted in his final memoir, Slowing Down, that people

have to be dead to be considered true legends, and they were calling Melly one when he was still alive, even though he was admittedly on his last legs, and the pens of scribes the world over were hovering over his half written obituaries. Now he's gone, and the ink has dried, legend is definitely valid.

George may be gone now, but his work and charisma lives on, as does his spirit, though not in a literal way of course, which would be ironic for the Humanist Atheist who denied God and anything beyond our mortal world. Without being sentimental, he left behind a sizeable body of work in print and on record, and in the hearts and memories of his many adoring fans. That said, even though George was a major celebrity in his life time, especially in the 70s and 80s, Melly is largely unknown to the new generation of millennial folk who prefer their idols brash and talentless, taking selfies at an alarming rate, finding so-called love on a desert island before a gawping nation of viewers, and filming themselves doing business on the toilet. Diana Melly, George's wife, said to me that interest in George has been gradually depleting, which suggests he is slowly fading into the annals of time. With that in mind, one of the aims of this book is to redirect younger people towards a figure who is not only very interesting indeed, but also worthy of their admiration. Whether it will succeed in that way is up for debate, but either way a celebration of his life's work is worthwhile and long overdue. Its other aim is to hopefully please the well established fans, who might feel the need to raise a glass once again for their fallen hero.

The book explores Melly's work in all areas; his books, his albums, his love of Surrealism, his other writings, his film scripts, and also his personal life. A look at the multiple mediums proves Melly's career was refreshingly varied, and his journey was long and winding. Let us not forget, he first came to prominence when he rode the greasy spoon fed trad-jazz boom of the 1950s, only to see his music career stalled by the arrival of The Beatles and the pop wave, putting jazz out of action for a decade or so until he re-emerged in the 1970s with John Chilton and a new band, ironically under the wing of the fab four's old press manager, Derek Taylor.

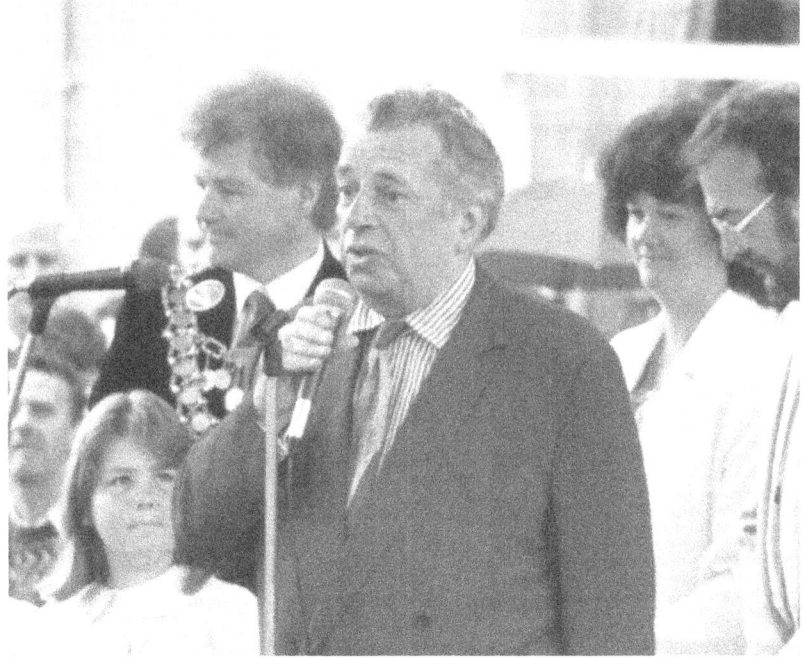

Melly at the Brecon Jazz Festival.

From then on, Melly enjoyed a successful ride as a live and recording artist, a juggling act which he managed to keep up solidly alongside his terrific broadcasting work, as well as writing projects, art criticism and other bits and bobs that tickled his fancy. Melly was an explorer of passions, some work related, others more personal. But whatever he took on, he gave it his all and never phoned it in.

This book then, is a plain and unfussy homage to George Melly, a loving tribute to a man I never met, but wish I had, and at times, especially given the research and delving I have partaken in recently, almost feel like I did. The latter feeling is, of course, a testament to the wonderful things he left behind for us to enjoy; the stories, the memoirs, and the music. And it's the music, funnily enough, which often gets sidelined in favour of his larger than life personality and often lewd shenanigans; which is a shame indeed, as he recorded some wonderful albums and was a massively popular live draw for several decades, a fact that may dim as the years go by.

I wrote this book while working on a documentary film about Melly, and have found the dual experiences deeply rewarding and endlessly fascinating. In many ways the book is the companion to the film, in that it features some of the same information and tone. But it is also a rough guide to a multi faceted life and body of work. He was a remarkable figure complete with his own folk lore and myth, which he chronicled himself in his life time. True, it's hard to ignore the strength of the Melly character, that almost cartoon like eccentricity that came to him so naturally - the boozing, the big hats, the zoot suits, the posh voice - but as his work was so well observed and always at the peak of its respective medium, it becomes easier to gaze past that persona and realise once again what a great mind he had, and how he applied it so excellently to every area of his working life. "George was a real grafter, he worked really hard," his one time girlfriend Louisa Buck told me, and a look at his records, books, TV work, live concerts, radio appearances and various articles proves that.

George wrote volumes of memoir, a colourful bibliography of art history, jazz, sexual shenanigans and intimate recollections, some very detailed and precise. I will not try to replicate every memory and occurrence of his life here, for that would be pointless. After all, you could just pick up one of his memoirs if you wanted to revisit those wonderful stories. I go through his life, sure, but the main aim is to explore his work, though autobiographical information is also essential to the progress of his life. So take a ride with me on the Mellymobile, but make sure you fasten your seat belt.

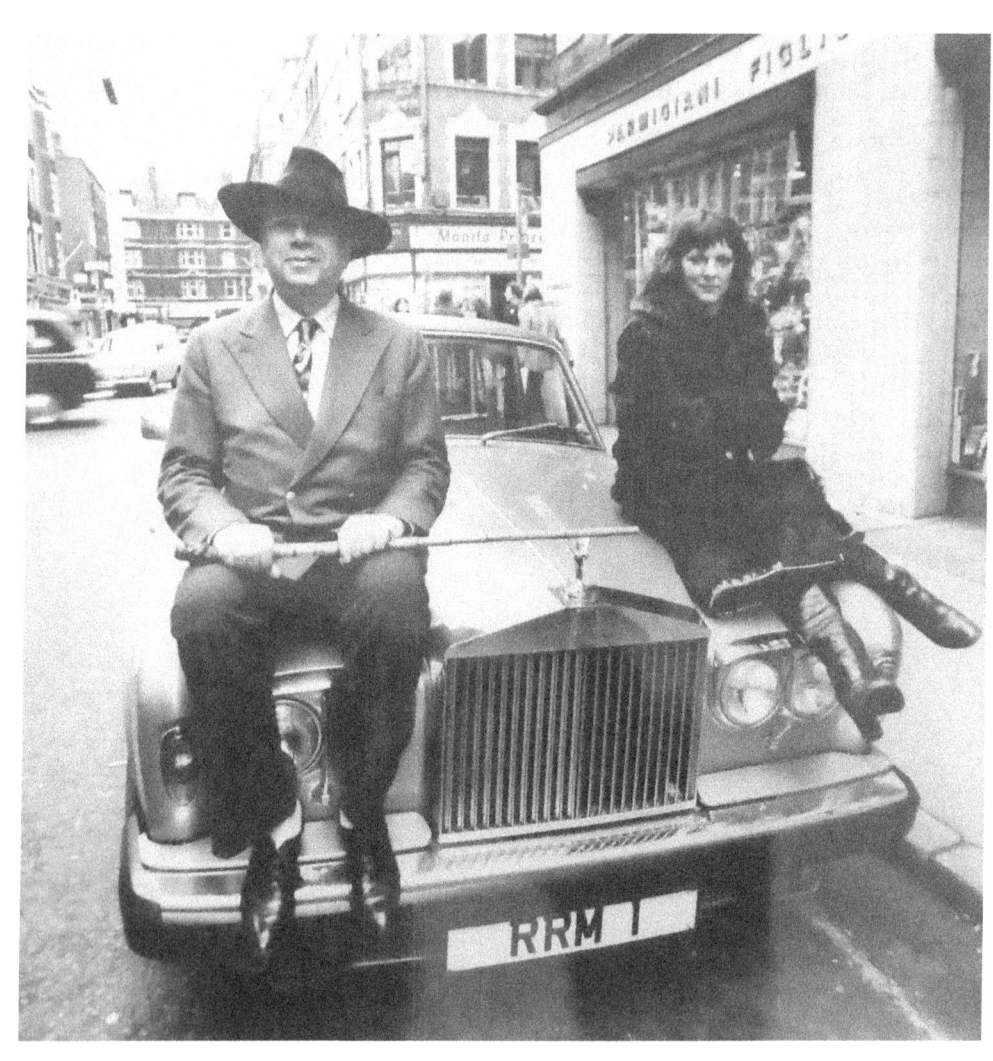

George and Diana Melly, early 1980s.

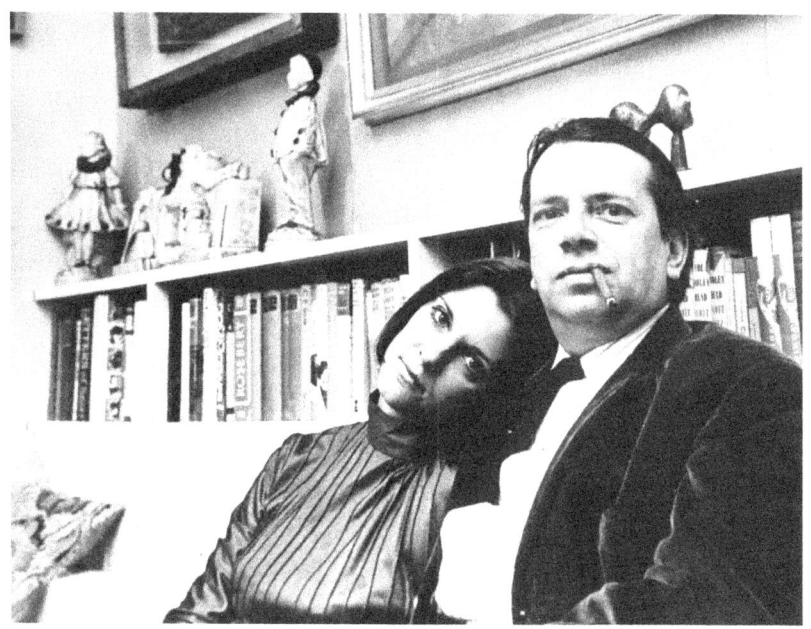

DIANA MELLY LOOKS BACK

Diana and George met in the early sixties and were married soon after. They strode on through the decade together as bohemian members of the in crowd. But things changed over night it seems in the early seventies when their marriage was declared open. Though they no longer had an intimate physical relationship after this, they remained a married duo ("They had an understanding," as their son Tom put it), with Diana acting as a kind of arranger for Melly's dizzying, increasingly busy life.

In the latter months, when George grew ill, Diana gave her all and began to care for him. She learned that a new found respect was earned in the final months, weeks and days. All this was put on film for the classic documentary George Melly's Last Stand, a shockingly candid glimpse into his illness and death. In the end, she says she was happy with George, content to simply look after this "great" and "charismatic" man.

"Three years before he died," Diana wrote in her brilliant memoir Strictly Ballroom, "I just thought his behaviour was becoming somewhat delinquent. He was losing credit cards – 14 in one month – because he couldn't remember his pin, which should have been easy as it related to his birthday. He would leave the front door open, lose his keys, and when travelling to London he would sometimes end up in Plymouth. I didn't take these episodes seriously. Then something happened that should have alerted me but still didn't. He was singing at Ronnie Scott's and when I called in at the club, admittedly unexpectedly, he didn't recognise me. A few weeks later (this was January 2005), his lung cancer was confirmed and I think I was putting his increasing memory lapses – which weren't just forgetting the names of his favourite film stars, Laurel and Hardy – down to his health, his whiskey and his medication. George had pills for his heart, high cholesterol, psoriasis, duodenal ulcers and a thyroid problem – and numerous inhalers for his lungs. But in March that year I stopped him in the street outside our house and again he failed to recognise me. When I told him my name, he asked if I was a cousin. We laughed it off, but when I told a friend, she said it wasn't funny and that she thought he had dementia. I went to my GP, who gave me the number of Admiral Nurses; she said they helped anyone worried about any aspect of dementia. I rang them and got through to Madeline; she listened carefully and said it sounded like vascular dementia with Lewy bodies."

Diana was there by his side, saying it was often a sad and depressing time, but that Melly punctuated this period with plenty of humour. His personality, though fading, made the ordeal more bearable.

"It's probably selfish and sentimental, but because I miss him, I sometimes wish he was still in his sitting room, in his hospital bed or even in a home and I was on my way to visit," Diana said eight years after his death. "When you miss someone it's not just the good bits and the happy times; you miss the whole person, the bad bits – and the sad bits."

I have been totally enthralled by the story of their marriage for a while now, so it was a thrill when I got a personal insight into their complex relationship. I rang Diana one warm Sunday afternoon, as my daughter banged on the door asking me to get her some juice and Diana's own granddaughter arrived at her house rapping on the door, and we spoke about life with and after George Melly. It was an interesting chat to say the very least. A few weeks later I took the trip to her home in Shepherds Bush, but this phone chat captured a lot of the complexities of their long and winding journey together.

You were married for 45 years. What is it like now, the fact that George has been gone for eleven years?

Well, it was very, very difficult at first, because he had such a big personality and such a big ego. You know, it was huge, the absence of it. But I think in time it was all right. I started to take up things I wouldn't have had time to take up before. And another thing, I always thought that I would be OK when he died, because he was sometimes so maddening to live with. But actually, when he died it was terrible, it was much worse than I thought it would be. I did miss him a lot. I sleep with the television on, and when he died I would quite often be waking up to the sound of George singing. For quite some time afterwards his voice was always on the television. I'd leave it on and suddenly George would be on some programme, and there he'd be singing.

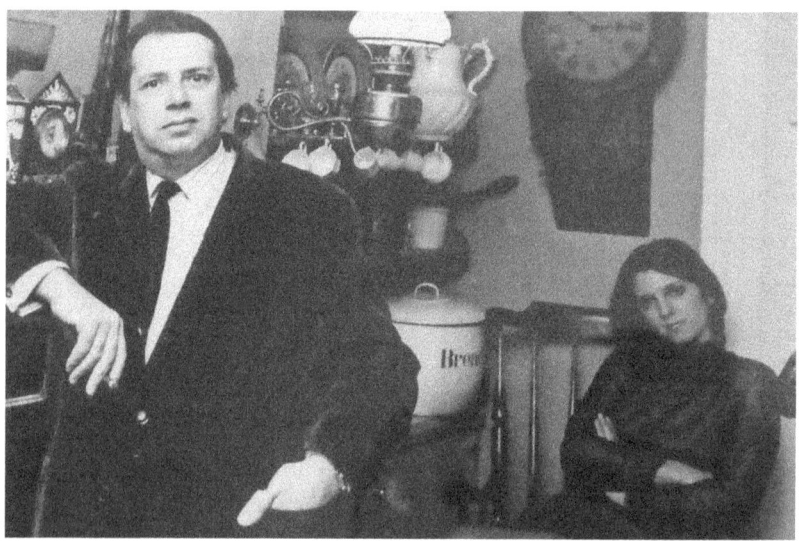

How do you look back on the time he was ill at the end?

I very much enjoyed looking after him when he was ill. When he became ill, he lost a lot of that huge personality. You know, in some ways he was much easier to live with, if that makes sense. So basically, that's what life has been like since... And I often think to myself, 'I wish I could ask George this' or 'I wish I could tell George that.' But when he was here, he was so knowledgeable I often didn't ask him because it was so irritating when he always knew the answer. And I didn't always tell him things because I felt he took over everything, so I liked to keep things secret. I mean, we'd been together since 1961, so we were together a very long time. We had, at times, a very difficult marriage, but other times it was also a very good one. And at the very end it was a good one. Very good. We both got older, obviously, and things got easier.

You were married, but you were also best friends in a way too. Or that's how it seems to me.

Yes I think so. But actually I'm not so sure. His interests were not always mine. I mean, I never really liked Surrealism, your thing... but I never much liked it. And I kind of preferred pop music. I liked the blues very much, but not always jazz. So I think in some ways we were very different, but we suited each other. You see, in some ways, I suited George because of my personality. I mean, if he was doing something fairly sort of posh, I was OK for that. And if he was doing something of the opposite I was OK for that too. He had two girlfriends at one particular time, one of them was a viscountess, so she was very, very posh, and he had another girlfriend who was a van driver, and she was not at all posh. So those two extremes didn't suit him. And I was in the middle, so I suited him very well, because I could cover both areas as it were.

More versatile!

Yeah.

But it seems now that, especially in the mainstream, culture doesn't have many or any characters like George. Why do you think there aren't people out there in the public world like him?

Well I'm not aware that they don't really. I mean he was a one off in his time, but it seems to me that there are still some amazing people around. Don't you think so?

Not as much, personally. That great eccentric cliché, which is true in his case, just doesn't seem to be around anymore. I mean, you might view it differently because you were married to him and with him for so long...

Well I am not sure I did think of him as being exceptional, but I realise now that I was wrong. He was very exceptional. I think something that people don't realise about him is that he was a very, very kind person. That's the thing that comes to mind most when I think about him, that he was so kind. I mean it is true that he was eccentric, especially in his clothes and everything... I mean, I go ballroom dancing a lot, which he probably wouldn't have liked, but there are some very eccentric people on the dance floor there. I mean, there is one man who goes and he often wears a pretty skirt and a flower in his hair. There are some eccentric people around still, so I definitely don't agree that there aren't any.

When it comes to all that extravagance and extroverted behaviour and dress and everything, how much of that was maybe a cover or a

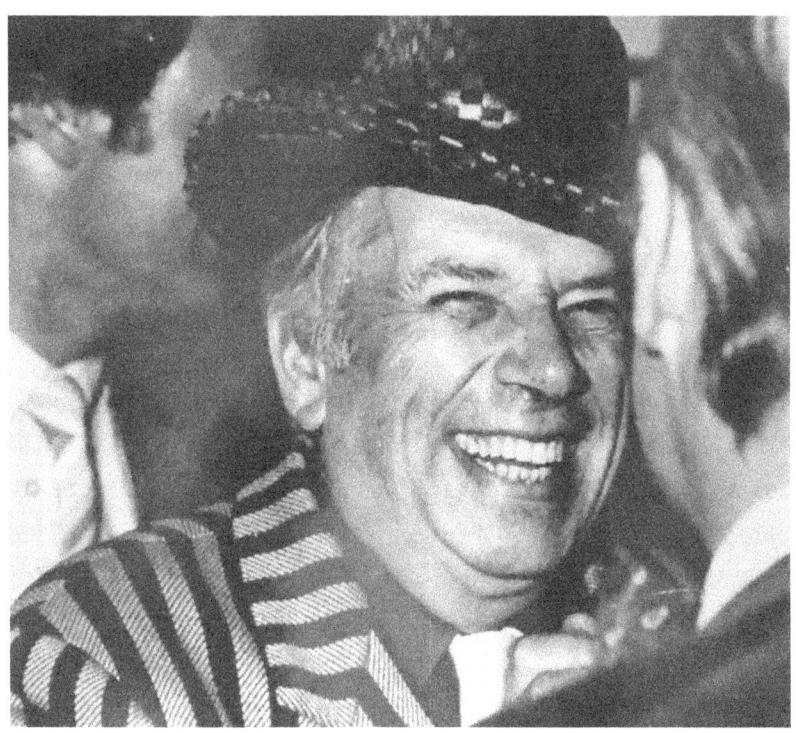

front, a performance if you like? Or was none of it that way? Was it all completely natural?

Well I think George was quite vain, and he loved being looked at, so his clothes were styled to be looked at. I mean he loved being photographed. I remember once when we were in Kenya together, and there was a show of all the different African people in their clothes, and without any encouragement from me, George went out and bought a kaftan. Towards the end of his life he wore kaftans all the time instead of the suits, because it was a lot less trouble to wear a kaftan. You see he didn't have any idea how to dress casually. He'd come down to dinner dressed in a suit, and I didn't want him to always come down for dinner in a suit. I'd rather he wear something more casual. So once he got into his kaftan phase that was more suitable for just sitting around in the kitchen.

They did suit him though didn't they, the kaftans?

They did, absolutely, yes!

I wanted to ask you about the documentary you made when George was dying, which was shown on the BBC after he died. There's a bit when you go see him perform live and you are very over come with emotion after having watched him. Is that when you realised the power he had singing live, or was there more to it than that?

No, I was just thinking how brave he was, because he was not at all well. I was overcome just how good he was even though he wasn't feeling well. I know I do say in the documentary that I wasn't feeling well, but I really wasn't, I did have the beginnings of flu and that always makes one a bit tearful. But it was somehow a very moving performance. Not all of his performances were, but that one was.

On the subject of his music, I think he helped bridge a gap between the mainstream world and the jazz world. He was definitely one of the people who made people get into jazz who might not have otherwise given it a chance. Do you agree?

He did, yes I think he did. But the trad world did that as well. Acker Bilk and Kenny Ball and all of them, their music became very popular indeed, more popular than George's music did. George never made much money from his music. I mean unless you actually write the song, you don't get much royalties really. You get paid for the performance, otherwise you don't get much. I remember I was always trying to get George to give up smoking. I remember in about 1985 when the doctors had cured the ulcer, they said he could do whatever he wanted, he could drink and eat as much as he liked, but they said 'One thing you mustn't do is to smoke again.' So George would give up. I helped him a great deal. I gave him colouring books and things. For a time his voice improved enormously. I thought, 'Well that will encourage him to stay off them.' In the end though that didn't last, it was too much for him and he started smoking again.

I was wondering if you ever listened to his music for pleasure at all?

Well, I never used to but I do more now. In fact one of the dances I go to on a Wednesday afternoon, the man there is a fan of George's and he often plays My Very Good Friend the Milkman. He slightly alters the timing of it sometimes so we can do a kind of slow fox trot to it. He's got two or three of George's songs, and I find that wonderful that one can dance to George's music, because I never thought I could.

That's quite interesting. I was reading his Mellymobile book today and he mentions the point in the mid 1970s when he suddenly became very popular as a jazz singer that his ego became bigger and he was much harder to live with. What are your thoughts on that?

Yes, I think his ego was always hard to live with. It got even bigger and bigger as time went on.

I am very interested in his Surrealist outlook too. He always said he was the world through a Surrealistic eye and he was a Surrealist to his finger nails. Do you think it really meant a lot to him?

Oh yes. I mean, the only time he ever got a bad review for something he was completely devastated. He had to stay in bed for three days. He and Jonathan Miller made a programme about Rene Magritte. When they showed it, they had edited it so that a scene with a painting with a ball rolling was cut, so it wasn't as good as it should have been. Also it got bad reviews. He was devastated and then went to bed. Apart from that I don't think he ever got a bad review for anything, not his books, his singing or anything.

Do you think younger people will get into him at all through his records?

No. He had a good voice obviously but he doesn't sound as good on CD or record or whatever as he did when he was giving performances. He was a performer much more than anything. He wasn't a great blues singer or anything. It was all in the performance.

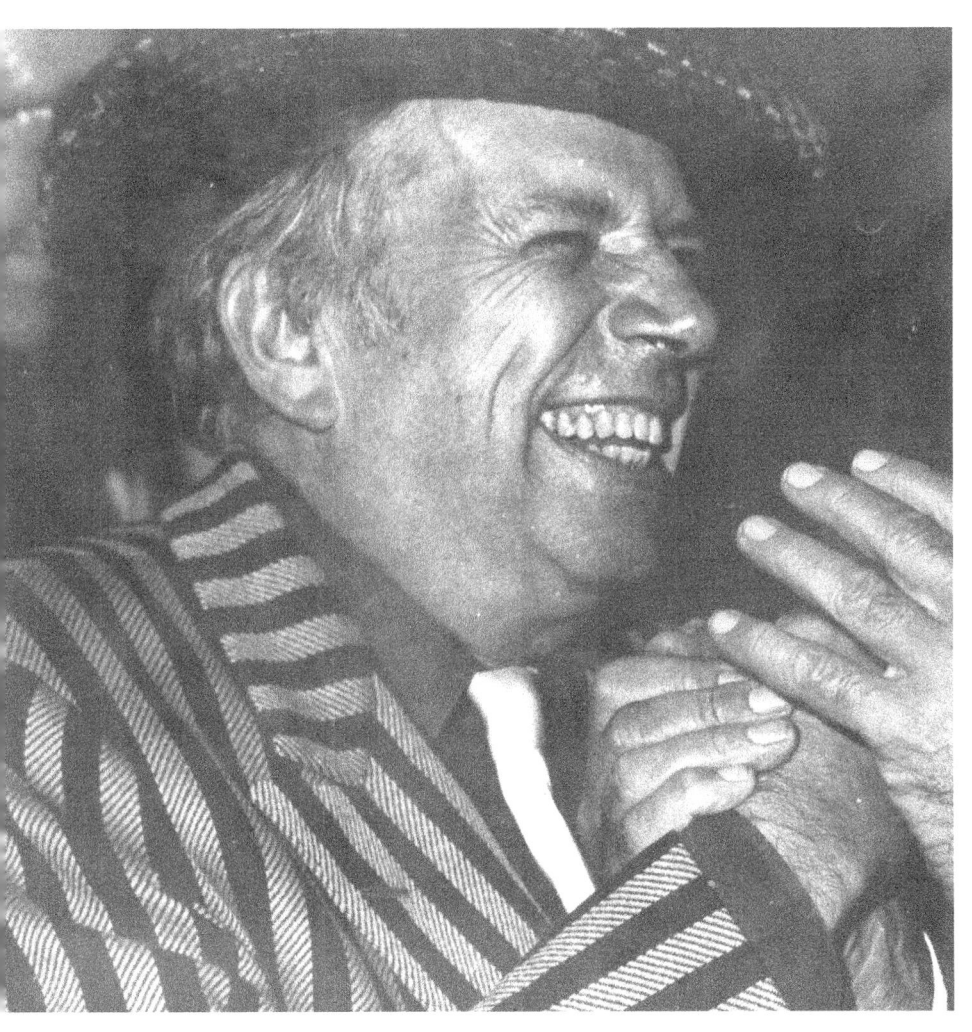

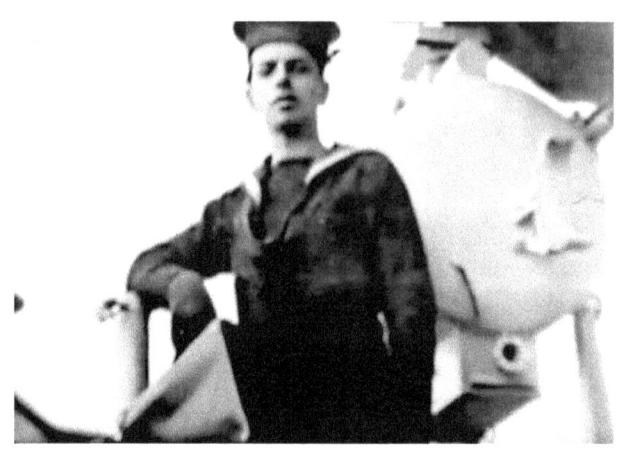

THE EARLY YEARS

"I don't mock my young naivety, I only envy it..."

Ever the myth maker, especially in regards to himself, Melly always made his life sound like an amazing surreal adventure, this loveable egomaniac who penned memoirs that made the ordinary into something extraordinary. As described in his childhood memoir Scouse Mouse, his formative years were eventful, warm and full of memorable occurrences. They took him from the womb and the streets of Liverpool, to the navy and working at a London art gallery. The first two decades or so are as fascinating as any other era of Melly's crammed, rich life.

Melly was born in Liverpool in 1926, not in his parents' house but in the larger home of his grandfather, The Grange on the Mersey. Before he could really take in his surroundings, Melly and his parents moved to a house on Ivanhoe Road, number 22 in fact. The house had a dairy behind it with its own cows, and pigs snaffled away in their sties. In the 1980s Melly wrote about returning there for a visit, asking for Tommy Hogg, the young man who had worked there all those years ago, and had been a ladies' man despite smelling of sour milk. Sadly, as the dairy boy informed him, he had recently died just before Melly's visit. Melly wrote, wonderfully I might add, "the pigs with their beady eyes grunted and strained up at us from their odoriferous sties." Even an ordinary thing such as a dairy from his childhood was made to sound like a dazzling Surrealistic moment from some strange dream.

George later spoke of some early memories, those sepia days of the mind's archive. As ever, he was wistful and beautifully sentimental about those long ago years. "I remember my mother or nanny taking me for walks and, to amuse me, rubbing her umbrella along railings," he said. "And I remember being in a garden in a house opposite where we lived in a street of Victorian terraced houses, and there was a maid who was a friend of our nurse, or nanny, hanging out washing. And the whiteness of the washing and the redness of her arms and the blue of the sky and the green of the grass..."

In poetic fashion, Melly also later pointed out the unreliable nature of memories and hazy nostalgia. Later, he recalled his first memory; he was sat in the passenger seat in a car beside his mother who drove them along a sea front. He described the scenario with such detail, recalling the perfect sky and water, but rounded off his recollection with the revelation, "the only problem is my mother never drove a car..." So much for memories...

His dad Tom was an easy going fellow and came from a well known and rather well off Liverpool family, big in business but perhaps lacking in personal passion. George's dad made money from the wool trade, though he did not enjoy his work. Meanwhile, Melly's Jewish mother, Maud, was active in Liverpool's amateur dramatics scene, and she spoke openly about her own early ambitions to be a star of the stage. She hung with the camp performers of the day, so Melly was exposed from a young age to homoscxuality, however disguised it may have been behind peacock-like flamboyance.

Some of the people Melly recalled from childhood were like caricatures form some great Surrealist novel; like Sily Sid, the harmless simpleton who used to stand up in the local cinema and declare "Give me a penny, I'm daft!" Other more terrifying figures included the paedophile who'd been castrated, but still tried to lure children to his house to see puppies, George's brother included.

His early holidays sound like strange, hazy dreams in themselves. Melly described his childhood trips to North Wales, staying in Llandudno, Angelsey, and the far reaches of Holyhead. Here he experienced fishing for the first time, a hobby which became an obsession until the end. Smoky, blurred images of his grandfather sum up the mood of 1930s holidays; the old man with his pocket watch, rolling up his trousers to paddle in the sea, the chauffeur waiting, reading the paper, while the three Melly chaps fished for hours. They'd buy worms from a man with a wooden leg in Holyhead. These places, which I have visited on various occasions, are indeed bizarre locations; they are bleak yet comforting, depressing yet strangely evocative. One can see why the Surrealist in George was both horrified and pleased by these slightly odd towns.

To say he became a man of words, Melly was not an early starter when it came to writing. "I was a very late developer, and I didn't really learn to read until I was seven," Melly told Paul Willetts, speaking of his early exposure to books. "But this is because people read to me, and I always found what they read more interesting than Janet and John or whatever you were meant to read. I suppose I was comparatively sophisticated about literature, but at the same time unable to go into it by myself. I had to depend on grown-ups who, luckily, had rather good taste or at least what one considers good taste in retrospect."

Melly was encouraged to be creative as a child, especially by his father, who repeatedly urged him to do as he pleased, and as he wanted. Edward Lear opened his heart to a world of Surrealism, and much later Lewis Carroll complimented his love of the extraordinary. His own writing though was harder to summon. "People liked what I wrote," he says of his childhood scribblings. "Gradually, I began to read more. My father read me Kipling's The Jungle Book. It's very important imaginatively to me, I think. I thought I might be a journalist on The Liverpool Daily Post or Echo which I saw every day, but I didn't really consider it very seriously. I thought I might be a genius like children often do. I thought I might write Ulysses or Proust. Always aiming high, not aiming at Somerset Maugham."

He was educated at Stowe School, and wrote vividly of the tyrannical head teacher, WW Twyne, an alcoholic who tended to go into manic episodes of rage. And it was in his earliest years - perhaps in part as an act of rebellion against the stiff conventions of the system he was born into - that he became fascinated with both jazz and Surrealism. Melly was open about his love affair for both, and seemed puzzled that there even had to be a connection in people's minds between the two interests. "People often say, What's the connection between Surrealism and jazz? And I say, Very little. But the things I value in the Surrealists and in jazz are exactly the same... For instance, Bessie Smith sang, My man's got teeth like the lighthouse on the sea, which is a pretty weird idea. Then the next line is Every time he smiles, he turns them lights on me. The initial image is extraordinary. There are many blues that have Surrealist

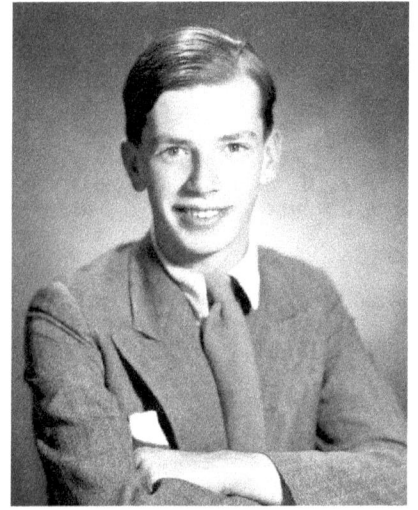

lines, but Surrealism and jazz are separate interests."

When he was around sixteen he came across a book about the art form by Herbert Read, and upon reading it, exploring Surrealism in its purest form, Melly said he felt as if he'd stumbled upon a world he always thought existed but didn't know how to access and understand. Surrealism offered a new truth, of the conscious and unconscious states being equally important, merged together, the everyday made extraordinary by a keen perception of one's surroundings. "A strange and often threatening garden," Melly dubbed it. "But a wonderful one nevertheless."

"I discovered Surrealism in the school holidays though a book by Herbert Read," Melly recalled. "I didn't understand much of the text, but I looked at the pictures. As I've often said, it felt like going through the wainscoat in Lewis Carroll and finding a magic kingdom that one had always known about but had never seen. That was what Surrealism did for me. It opened the key to another world."

Another Surrealistic incident which made him a loyal convert came when he visited Liverpool's Sefton Park as a young man, standing in the tropical house and chatting to wounded soldiers, many of whom were missing limbs. The sight of them smoking their cigarettes amidst the tropical plants triggered a feeling that the entire world around him was potentially surreal, whether you took notice or not. "He got a buzz out of it," his former girlfriend Elda Abramson told me, "that he only got again with Surrealism."

Melly then joined the navy. His life took a dramatic turn and he embraced what was then his definite homosexuality. As being gay was still a crime in the UK, Melly was certainly brave in his homosexual practices, but it was also common, so plenty of other young sailors were also walking the tight rope.

"According to documents released by the Public Record Office," Melly wrote in The Times in 2002, "dozens of explicit photographs of British sailors were found in a flat in Bermuda in 1969. Hundreds of sailors were involved in what is described as gross indecency. In response, commanding officers were ordered to 'stamp out this vice'. But the clampdown would have been 20 years too late to trap me. I joined up in 1944, at a time when I was about 95% gay. The 5% is accounted for in that around that time I went to bed with an attractive older woman at her invitation, but the deal included her husband, so perhaps the 5% is a little overgenerous." (More of this last sentence later.)

Melly recounts his activities with much detail in Rum, Bum and Condertina, a memoir released in the 1970s, when he was a married man, "straight" as it were, with children of his own. But Melly was not one to deny his past. In fact he looked back with fondness and recalled the many tales with glee, nostalgic wonderment even. Though he never saw combat or had his life put at serious risk, it was another valuable term in the school of life.

Remarkably enough for the time, his parents did not mind he was gay so much. His father, a rich man by anyone's judgements, was very understanding, and his mother wasn't fussed about his sexuality either; in fact she even encouraged it, though she did think that his tendency to go after both sexes was just plain greedy.

"Well, the homosexual part pleased her rather than the bisexual part," he told Alastair McKay. "She was something of a fag hag. She adored homosexuals, except for my father, and my father was perfectly tolerant about that. He didn't mind when it was obvious I was going to be a queen, and he didn't mind when I stopped being a queen and turned to the other sex."

After his navy days at the back end of the war, Melly met up with the English Surrealists upon their invitation, reading them one of his surreal poems in the Barcelona restaurant in London, throwing the cutlery into the air and being officially embraced by the leader of the English Surrealists, the Belgian artist and gallery owner, ELT Mesens. "It was very dangerous," Eileen Agar recalled, who was present at the time, "but it was by then getting very dull."

"The Barcelona restaurant was one of those mountain caves where we brigands of the imagination were preparing to march against the forces of reason and overthrow those obscene myths whose function was to cretinise humanity," was how George romanticised the establishment where the English Surrealists gathered. It seems fitting that Melly was so interested in joining a group which was on its last legs, limping unfashionably into the 1950s, the era of modern art, with the pre echoes of pop art all around.

"His attempt to revive Surrealism during the post-war indifference to the movement was a complete failure," Melly recalled in 2006 of Mesens' inspired but doomed mission. "The intellectuals (many of them gay) who had found it "amusing" before the war thought of it now as old hat. Only a few young poets and a handful of painters remained faithful, and they had very little money to keep a commercial venture going. Neo-romanticism was the new fashion, spiced up by a little decorative Cubism and pretty colours. It was all we could sell, and later, in desperation, ELT allowed artists to hire the rooms. Meanwhile, in the cellars languished masterpieces by Ernst, Tanguy, Arp, Delvaux, etc - and especially Magritte, ELT's almost lifelong friend and supporter."

Still, his association with Mesens had its upsides. George ended up working in Mesens' gallery, becoming exposed to all kinds of art and artists. Typically, Melly even enjoyed some rumpy pumpy with him and his wife (all this is recounted in Melly's memoir of this period, Don't Tell Sybil), but Surrealism was their true passion together. Melly invested in art, being given 900 pounds by his father (a lot of money at the time) to put it in the right place. He was loyal enough to buy from Mesens' gallery. Instead of opting for what was valuable at the time, Melly bought what he fancied. By this stage Surrealism was considered old hat. "Not by me" he said, buying among other things a Magritte and a drawing by Picasso. Magritte was another early key influence, when he saw Viol (The Rape) and fell in love with its air of mystery. He was later the proud owner of it.

Melly, Mesens and Sybil went to bed together a few more times, but it soon petered out. George and Sybil made love once while Mesens was away and bizarrely, after the threesomes stopped, Mesens and Melly continued partaking in private sexual experimentation together. One time they even masturbated on to a plate and fiendishly got on their knees to lap it up like cats. Melly was later ashamed of the incident (though not ashamed enough to omit it from his memoirs), calling it the most melancholy and depressing moment of his erotic life. He did not find Mesens attractive, but partook in such activities almost out of pity, obligation and respect, because he knew how much Mesens enjoyed it all. Another time they both went with a plump middle aged Belgian whore. Melly found it a rather pathetic copy of the affectionate threesomes they had enjoyed with Sybil. There was something sad about the whole situation and both men later felt ashamed.

This aside, he was rather useless at the gallery, always turning up late to open the doors and getting things wrong. His main tasks were answering the phone, posting invitations for exhibitions and writing letters for Mesens, all of which he often messed up. It was his lack of punctuality though that enraged the hard drinking Belgian the most. Coming away from the job three years later, Melly thought the main thing he had learned was how to hang an exhibition decently.

Through Mesens' influence and status within the Surrealist circles, Melly even had the chance to meet his Surrealist idol, Andre Breton. His first trip to Paris in the early 1950s, when he "borrowed" 50 pounds from his mother, had been a mostly deflating, boring affair. He made empty love with prostitutes and nearly got scammed by them; he ran into Lucien Freud and saw his birds; he roamed the streets, glum and ghost like, ignored by the Parisians; he stalked the Surrealist landmarks but found no rewards in doing so. It was a wash out in many ways, though Melly went back home pretending it had been a triumph, that he had made passionate love to the most beautiful whores (in reality, the one he came across was older, while her "sister" tried to steal his wallet, in a run down, seedy hotel), enjoyed the best jazz and had a fabulous week all round.

Later, Melly went back to Paris with a note from Mesens to guide him to Breton's home, which he vowed to visit this time. Writing in his book Paris and the Surrealists, Melly described his meeting with Breton with such excitement that he had to admit he was coming across as a schoolgirl who'd met her favourite pop star. "But this is how I felt," he said. Though Breton spoke no English and Melly no French, they somehow communicated and got along fine. Breton even invited his young fan to a restaurant where he would meet other Surrealists, younger men he was not aware of. Still, it was a thrill to sit there with Breton at the head of the table, even if Melly did imagine the other seats being occupied by the likes of Salvador Dali and Max Ernst, thirty years earlier in the glory days.

George left the London Gallery but kept his friendship with the Mesenses alive until ELT's death in the early 1970s. It wasn't always a pleasant friendship to say the least, and Mesens was certainly a foreboding character in some regards, but George had fond memories of this time, his coming of age so to speak. But from here on, he did not have the safety net of the relatively lenient Surrealist Mesens to fall into. He was on his own out in the world now and he had to choose a path. As it turned out, the path was jazz...

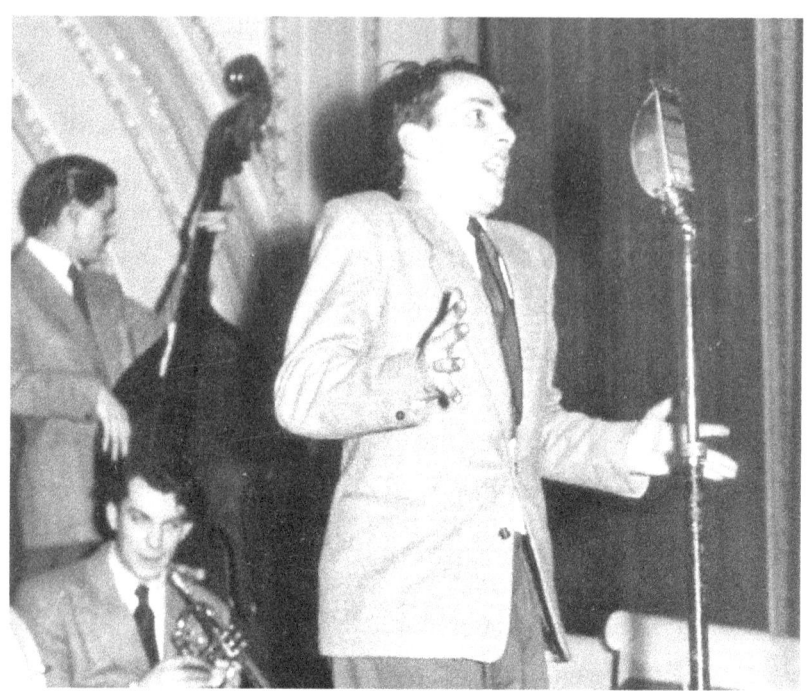

MELLY AND THE TRAD JAZZ BOOM

George Melly's love of jazz began with an admiration verging on worship for the old black jazz blues singer Bessie Smith. This was a life long adoration which lasted until the end of his life. Even as an old man, he ensured he listened to at least one or two Bessie tracks on a morning. "She's my goddess really," he admitted.

"It was the fact that she was at the edge of two worlds – folk-blues, and sophisticated vaudeville singing," Melly said, explaining his love of Smith. "But she sung it with an immense sincerity. You felt she meant every word. She revealed herself in an extraordinary way. And her vocal tricks were wonderful – breaking notes in two and diving down. She was just a great artist."

He explained his love to the Independent: "I'm reading a book about Bessie Smith at the moment, written like a love letter by Jackie Kay, who's a black Glaswegian woman poet. I believe her to be completely sincere because I also fell in love with Bessie Smith while being just a middle-class public schoolboy from Liverpool. She was my first big influence. When I started singing in the late Forties, I used to actually ask her to come down and enter me, her spirit that is. It was pretty far out. And I still play Bessie's songs every day. I have all her tapes. I play two of them while I'm getting dressed, or three if I've got a hangover. I know them all backwards and they never lose their magic."

The fact that Melly connected with her so early ensured that she remained one of his greatest passions in life. Indeed, even in his final concerts he was still singing the Bessie blues, and wonderfully too I might add. He managed to capture her passion, her depth, her emotion, and a lot of her power. She had died before he'd even discovered her, but that only added to his mythical view of Smith.

With Andre Breton and Bessie Smith as his two idols, Melly set out on a life of full awareness and liberation. Before long, and inevitably so given his passion for the genre, Melly entered the jazz world, just as the New Orleans Revival began to take hold in the late forties and early fifties. After dilly dallying around for a short period, Melly teamed up with Mick Mulligan and his band, becoming a firm fixture on the live scene, going up and down the country performing to avid trad jazz fans and becoming something of a cult figure, known for his lewd lyrics and eccentric on stage performances, as well as his wild behaviour off stage. If anything though, the most impressive thing about him was that he could channel the soul of Bessie Smith on stage, even though he could not have been more different from her in terms of their respective backgrounds and appearances. Still, the jazz blues was in his soul.

Undoubtedly, the name George Melly first became known to the public, or sections of the public at least, during this boom, in which the Dixieland style of the turn of the century found new popularity, most notably in London, but also in the provinces. Through jazz, it could be said, Melly let out his Dadaistic impulses, the spontaneity which is in some regards a complete contrast to the psychological, subversive and logical world of Surrealism. Going wild on stage, especially in the free and liberating genre of jazz, was a kind of Dada release. George, more than any other UK jazzer of the era, summed up what it was to be wild with his on stage antics, flamboyance and off stage activities transcending all expectations and rules. He even found that Dada could get him out of rough scrapes while on the road. One night after a gig up north some local hooligans cornered him with broken bottles. Things were about to turn nasty, but Melly suddenly began to recite Kurt Schwitter's Ursonate poem at the top of his lungs, as a kind of gut reaction, and before very long they had turn and fled.

As a cultural boom, there was a carefree, fast and high living excitement to this new jazz movement that appealed to George. It seems he was born just at the right moment to fully immerse himself in jazz and all it had to offer him. Speaking in 1983 about what he might have done if he'd been born thirty years later in the fifties, George said, "I wouldn't have been a jazz singer — I don't think I'd have been exposed to it. I might have still written but I'd have been a lot more pessimistic. We've reached the end of the time when the world was going to be changed through love, hallucinatory drugs etc. We felt that the individual then could change things by sitting down in Trafalgar Square or marching to Aldermaston. And I think kids just don't feel that anymore, they feel very cynical about the possibility of anyone affecting anything. They still go marching, yes, but I do feel that there just isn't the feeling that things are going to change for the better."

For George, jazz fit him perfectly, and seeing as he was in his prime during the trad boom, he seems to have identified with the idealism and naivety of that era more than any other. Unlike the sixties, which were LSD fuelled times of often misguided optimism, or the angry 70s, a time of poverty, strikes and rage, Melly's fifties were an era to let loose, have fun and maybe think about social changes, though not obsess over them.

The trad jazz boom came at just the right moment in time. After all, it wasn't even a decade since the Second World War had grounded to a halt, and the UK, particularly London, still bore the scars of the air raids. "Everything was peeling," George said on the BBC documentary Smokey Dives. Good old fashioned fun, consequence free and wide eyed fun at that, was very much in demand after a decade of gloom, devastation and explosive bombardment.

"Jazz was immensely romantic for us," Melly said. "The difference between jazz and pop is that pop was a thing connected with the present whereas jazz was a nostalgic look back to a sort of idealised paradise. Some of it came out of public school, some out of housing estates. The mass of it was suburban, probably university students from suburban houses."

In the annals of British popular music, trad jazz is often seen as a dirty term; and worse still, sometimes totally neglected and written out of history. The Beat Boom of the 1960s is regarded to be the moment Britain first kicked into action after the war, even though 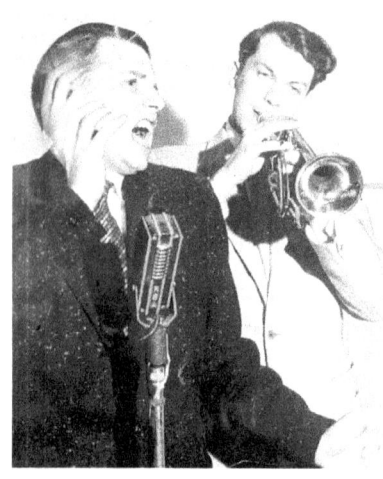 The Beatles arrived on the charts a whole 18 years after the end of World War 2. Music historians, for some reason - perhaps because it fits their romanticised view of pop becoming a serious art form in the 1960s - choose to hop over the 50s as a time for serious social and musical change, painting the era as a drab, grey and dull wash out, lifted only by the arrival of Elvis and rock and roll, and on our own shores, the emergence of skiffle. The fifties then, are often seen as the warm up to the revolutionary sixties, apparently the first time Britain shot into Technicolor after the greyness of the war. George Harrison once said that The Beatles saved the world from boredom. He was right in some regards, especially in America where they were suffering a down beat time in the wake of JFK's assassination just before the fab four arrived there like heroes from another time or planet. But one cannot help feel that journalists, historians and even the musicians themselves from the 1960s are doing one genre something of a disservice - and that genre is British Traditional Jazz.

Writing for the Guardian, Philip Clark summed up most people's attitudes towards trad jazz rather well, writing, "To the uninitiated, it might sound like the very embodiment of British eccentricity to be filed under Gilbert and Sullivan, morris dancing and re-enacting the battle of Culloden over a wet bank holiday weekend. But to those teenagers and twenty somethings who danced the night away, listening to bands led by Humphrey Lyttelton and Acker Bilk in clubs dotted around Soho during the mid-1950s, British traditional jazz would provide stolen moments of escapism from grimy post-war London. Despite that, trad's fate has been to be mocked for being hopelessly retrospective, a situation not helped by its collapse, away from Barber and Lyttleton's scholarly approach, towards novelty records and the twee theatrics of Acker Bilk's bowler hats."

In our cynical modern times, the idea of revitalising an old time musical form seems rather naive and twee, but there was actually something very gritty and raw about the fifties trad jazz scene that makes it utterly fascinating, especially when one delves in and discovers the sordid and wonderful things that went on amidst the booming jazz and wild cavorting.

Melly's first jazz gig as a punter, one that awakened him to its true charms, was at the Scala Theatre when he was young, watching the Graeme Bell band. He dubbed it "real jazz," before adding "I came out of that concert a changed man." It all started for George as a performer when he met fellow jazz nut Mick Mulligan, while accompanying a friend to an audition for Mick's band. George couldn't play an instrument, but like his hero Bessie Smith, could belt out a song with enthusiasm and provoke a certain atmosphere when he did so. Mick didn't need a singer, but felt obliged to take Melly on as his vocalist because he seemed so insistent that he do so. When George turned up he had impetigo from a rusty razor blade, was half unshaved and smeared with ointment. "What a lecherous looking bastard" said Mick, handing him a cigarette and hiring him immediately.

Their first gig was at a youth club, where there was no microphone available for George. He acted fast and sang into an empty biscuit tin. "The lads listened politely," Melly recalled. "After about half an hour a small boy poked his head round the door of the recreation room and shouted 'Chocolate biscuits in the canteen'. Rationing was still in force and the whole room emptied for the rest of the evening."

For George, life in the Mick Mulligan band was feral and uncensored. "I did all that I wanted on the road," he said with a sense of achievement. "We all did in the Fifties. Stayed in awful digs. But they were rather amusing, too, in retrospect. Ate fried rubbish. Seduced who would be willing to be seduced in the scrubber belt as we called it. And so on. A good time was had by all. What was that joke? She was a good time that was had by all. Dorothy Parker, yes."

George's view on jazz was that it shook up the system, attempted to tear up the rule book and set the country free from its rigours, traditions and isms. "Disaffection hasn't got that much to do with jazz," he once said. "It has to do with not looking like mummy wanted and not living like mummy wanted and screwing more than mummy wanted and certainly drinking much more than mummy wanted, but it didn't have much to do with disaffection. I mean within it one could say there were people who were Labour supporters, a few communists, a few fascists even. But the mass of people were vaguely Labour inclined, certainly pro-black which was a very important element because the people we admired the most were black. It wasn't to do with organised disaffection, it was more to do with thumbing one's nose at the bourgeois motives."

Seeing as no live footage of Melly and Mulligan exists from the 1950s (although there are some fabulous photographs preserving that era), one has to turn to recordings to get an idea of what they were about. As Diana Melly mentioned to me, nothing that Melly did on record could hope to match his live appearances. He was a performer through and through, while it was essential to see him as well as hear him to take in the whole picture. That said, some of the recordings he made in the 1950s remain splendid, even today when some of the records are nearly seventy years old.

In the early 1950s, Melly recorded as George Melly Trio for Tempo Records, cutting the single Rock Island Line, grouped with the B side, Send Me to the 'Lectric Chair. It is incidentally the B side which remains the most interesting today, a song covered by his hero Bessie Smith but written by Fletcher Henderson. A dark and foreboding introduction starting with deathly piano and rolling drums gives way to an authentic and wonderfully sung take by Melly, sounding like an old New Orleans crooner from the turn of the century. Graphic as it is (George sings of cutting his girl's throat) he actually makes it a rather pleasant ditty, if one ignores the lyrics of course. The song was banned at the time, and a BBC manager wrote of George that he was "a rather hungry looking dark young man of untidy and rather effeminate appearance in black trousers and windcheater." I am sure Melly himself agreed with every word.

Much of the 50s singles and EPs have been gathered together on CD compilations and vinyl sets over the years, including The World of George Melly, Sporting Life and George Melly Sings Doom. Going through the recordings takes one back to another time; not necessarily the 50s trad jazz scene in the UK, but elsewhere, further back in fact, for the songs conjure up an old world feel and images of an exotic nature. He may have worshipped the old black legends, but on record he sounded just like one himself.

In 1952 Melly teamed up with Alex Welsh and his band for the Frankie and Johnny single, easily one of the finest cuts Melly put down in the 50s. It was coupled with a solid B side too, often put on Melly compilations, I'm Down in the Dumps. Though he recorded it

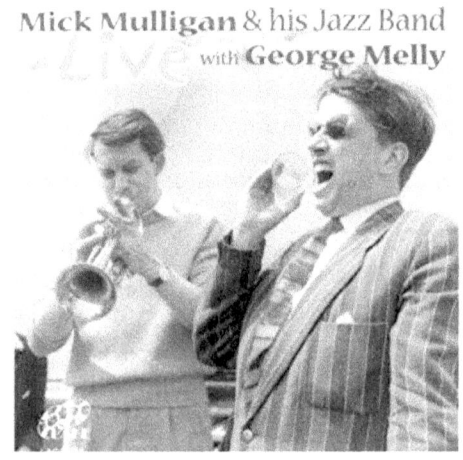

again and much better in the future, the early 50s recording of Kitchen Man, another Bessie Smith classic, is superb, with Melly's voice sounding rich and extremely expressive. Despite, or perhaps due, to the aged recording, the song has a terrific vibe to it, even if it's a world away from the more crisp recordings he made of it with John Chilton and Digby Fairweather in later stages of his jazz career.

Melly recorded some marvellous EPs and singles in the 1950s, including the brilliant 4 track set Nothing Personal, George Melly Sings the Blues. But my personal favourite music from this era, perhaps mostly for ambience and mood, is the 1959 LP Meet George Melly with Mick Mulligan, later reissued by Pye in the mid 1970s at the height of Melly's fame. Something about the album captures - at least I can guess so - what it was like to see George, Mick and company back in the day. It makes you want to light a fag (and I don't even smoke!) and fill your glass with whiskey.

There are some fabulous versions of old jazz standards here, such as the opening Mama Don't Allow It, with George on typically loose form. All Of Me is a beautiful bit of old time jazz, beautifully played with some great solos and a solid groove to it. Melly has taken a step back here, probably having a swifty at the bar, and giving the musicians room to shine alone.

Rocking Chair is marvellous too, perhaps the highlight of the record for me, where Melly's voice matches the towering stature of 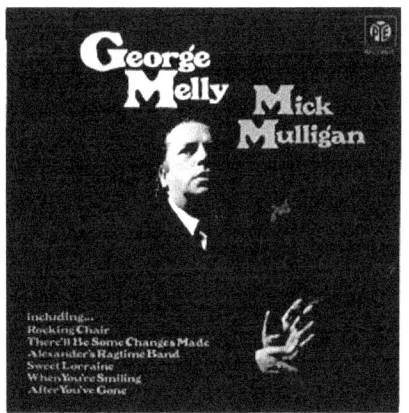 Louis Armstrong in sheer charisma alone. Melly would record this again, just as memorably near the end of his life in fact, but there's a vitality here that cannot be ignored. Melly sounds every bit the star he most certainly was to the trad jazz audience.

There'll Be Some Changes Made has a jaunty swing to it, with a deep Melly vocal getting straight to the matter. There are other nice instrumental spots too, such as Girl of My Dreams, but the album is at its best when Melly is present and up front. The great man isn't messing around on Alexander's Ragtime Band, and the kooky After You've Gone, which also features some superb guitar work and general instrumentation. I also love the smoothness of Sweet

Lorraine, which is probably Melly's finest bit of vocal on the whole record, a rich, penetrating and very expressive piece of performance, channelling the old masters with ease and class.

Adding to the sweetness of the music are the authentic sounds of jazz loving drinkers chinking glasses at their tables and raucously laughing in their gathered circles as the band play on. It's essential stuff in my view which effortlessly conjures up a whole other era, one which is now long gone.

To accompany the music of this time, the rough and ready trad jazz standards often played with ineptitude due to lack of rehearsals but enough enthusiasm to ensure they measured up to ten good bands, one must read Melly's own jazz memoir, Owning Up (I am sure most if not all readers will have enjoyed this book at some stage) where he recounts these glory years wonderfully. Mulligan and Melly's antics were brought to life in this excellently written journey through jazz and sleaze, though Mulligan could not help but later remark, "George owned up about everyone but himself."

Though Melly does dish out the details on others, especially of Mick's stormy marriage and often volatile behaviour, he doesn't exactly spare himself, and the book is full of wonderful scenarios, memories and images so startling they remain burned into the brain. The bus crash the band suffers around half way through is particularly vivid, with George even shouting out, "This is it then," believing his life is about to end as the bus tumbles over, bodies and instruments floating around against all odds of gravity, before heading into the water. Perhaps my favourite image, though it's rather unsettling in itself, and using the word favourite seems a little sick, is of the boy with the large head gazing into a bucket of maggots. There are plenty of juicy tales in it, lots of boozing, dodgy characters (the various van drivers working for the band are a real rogue's gallery), greasy spoon cafes and sleaze by the bucket load. As a portrait of the scene it's just got to be unmatched, for Melly leaves in all the less savoury stuff that others writers might have leapt over or swept slyly under the carpet. Still, the music also does a good job of conjuring the atmosphere of those smoky dives.

This was a wonderful era for British music, a moment of glory for the often side lined jazz genre, and a legendary time in Melly's career. It has taken on a mythical quality in the Melly world, and indeed most of the musicians George jammed and partied with are dead now. But in listening to these recordings, you can close your eyes, lay back and transport yourself back to another time, another place, an era of innocence, and good old fashioned fun with little or no regard for consequences or the world outside. Or if that's too pretentious for you, you can turn the record up to full volume, dance your bollocks off until you're sweating like a mad chimp and do so until 7 a.m., just as George Melly, the band and the ravers did all those years ago, crawling out of jazz clubs drenched to the bone, high on substances and squinting in the harsh light of a new day. Escapism is what it was about, and it still can be today, if that's what you're looking for.

By the time the 1960s had started though, Melly and many others were losing interest in the trad jazz scene. Melly had been one of the popular stars and singers of the movement, but as rock and roll was coming in with the force of a juggernaut, jazz was looking even older hat than it had before. It was a turning point for him. Melly admitted his shameful vanity when he recalled a time he queued up for a blues gig at the start of the 1960s, with hundreds of other people, and was sad to say no one recognised him. The tide had turned...

"After 12 years I was tired of staying in horrible digs, eating filthy fried food," he said to the New York Times in 1978. "I got out just before I would have been forced out by the arrival of the Beatles."

Melly's exit from the jazz scene is always made out to be a sudden one, as if he woke up one morning and decided jazz was out and writing was in. Not the case. As he writes in his books, he was already working on the text for Trog's Flook comic strips at this stage. "I think they asked me because it sounded so extraordinary that somebody in the jazz world could write," Melly said. "We were meant to be morons. A few of us were."

As 1960 turned to 61, he and the boys began to play less gigs. Constant touring was replaced by one weekend a month and the odd local gig. It wasn't just a one sided decision either. Mick Mulligan told Melly he'd had enough of the touring too, and he wanted a more settled, quiet life. "Trad jazz became rather boring and repetitive," George said years after his retirement from the jazz scene in the early 1960s. "You know, played in every pub by gynaecologists on their night off. It was fine to drink to, but unsubtle."

As it happens, 1961 turned out to be a vital year for Melly. Firstly his dad died, his first marriage began to dissolve, enthusiasm for band life was waning and Melly got a very important writing job for Queen Magazine, an insider's view of the jazz world. "On the road," Melly wrote in his piece, "ten years of it. I seem to have spent a life time looking out of grimy windows in digs at backyards in the rain. Weeds, rotting iron, collapsing outhouses."

Melly's picture is not one of glamour, and these sentences alone are enough to explain exactly why he had had enough at that point. After all, it had been over a decade of on the road excess and hedonism. Melly called the article the key to his release from the tiresome jazz scene, as popularity and interest slid in favour of rock and pop. He acted as compere for various jazz nights, but more writing work was coming in. In almost perfect timing, in the autumn of 62 when band activity was petering out all together, he met Diana, the woman he would marry a year later. Now a writer's life awaited him for the next decade or so.

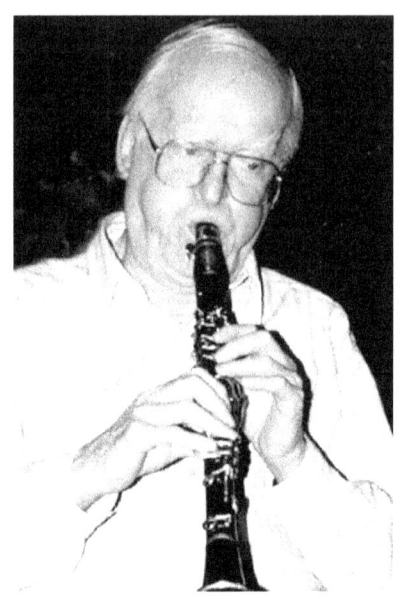

WALLY FAWKES ON GEORGE MELLY

It's not often I get to chat to genuine legends, a word used for just about everyone these days. But Wally Fawkes, now aged 94, is one where the word genuinely fits the man in question. Born in Canada, Fawkes always had an interest in comic books and cartoons, but his first job was during the war, painting the roofs of factories in camouflage tones to hide them from bombers. He won an art competition during the war run by the Daily Mail and ended up getting work there providing illustrations from 1945 onwards. He also struck up his passion for jazz, playing in war time bands and eventually joining the legendary Humphrey Lyttelton band. Around this time he took on the pseudonym Trog, and quit professional jazz in 1956 to give the cartooning the full attention it required. He provided strips and caricatures for The Spectator, Private Eye and the New Statesman, with George Melly as his text writer.

I rang Wally's home one Monday afternoon, his wife answering the phone and disturbing Wally from listening to an audiobook on his headphones. He then came to the phone, a gentle sounding and good humoured bloke, very easy and nice to talk to.

So Wally, you knew George all those years. How would you sum up his character in the early days of the 1950s?

He didn't really change. George was always larger than life, which made everybody else seem smaller than life. He had a terrific sort of life force with him, incredible enthusiasms. I remember saying to him once, after some outrageous bit of behaviour, 'If only you could overcome your shyness, there'd be no end to your possibilities.'

I'm interested in how you both ended up working on the Flook comic strips together, with you doing the art work and George writing the text.

Well Trog was my pen name. Humph had been writing them for me before then. I had got to the stage that playing in Humph's band, with the increasing amount of touring while keeping the strip going, and other political cartoons emerging, I was finding it difficult to keep all the things together. I knew for a fact that the playing was fun, enormous fun, and I loved it, but it was not a career. I knew my real work was the cartooning. I could do it from home, for a start. You can't play in a band from home, not without the neighbours complaining. So I quit Humph's band in 56 to spend more time with the cartooning. So Humph was doing the Flook strip, and by releasing him from the strip, it enabled him to really get on the road in a big way. So it became more than full time. The manager of the Mick Mulligan band, for whom George was singing, was a friend, and I was telling him about this and he said 'Why not get George in to do the strip?' I knew George as a sort of outlandish and marvellous man, but I hadn't thought of him for the job. But of course he was brilliant. He brought to it the social world that he inhabited, because he liked them but he mocked them mercilessly. He loved the minor aristocracy. And he really bit the hand that fed him, and I am like that too. That was perfect for the strip and perfect for the time. The middle fifties was when the social scene was beginning to unravel. You can't think now, but the Prime Minister was called Sir Alec Douglas-Home. But we accepted all that. Then the whole thing changed. The revolution I suppose, the revolution in the theatre, all before rock and roll and pop took over, to put an end to us (jazzers).

I suppose the jazz thing came back again bigger in the 1970s didn't it though?

Oh yeah. George came back too, but it was different, it was to do with his personality. If he'd been a trumpet player or a trombonist it would have been different, but it was his singing, which was extravagant to say the least. It made me wince every now and again. It wasn't my favourite sound, George's voice. (Laughs)

But you and George were playing with John Chilton for a bit weren't you, in the early 1970s?

Yeah that's right, we were playing at Merlin's Cave, near King's Cross every Sunday, around mid day.

What were those shows like?

Oh, fabulous! Tremendous. They were lovely, absolutely lovely. And children were allowed in too. You couldn't get in unless you had a child with you. They used to blow their coke bottles at us in retaliation as we blasted away. And the visiting Americans used to come in. And then George started coming in, and that put an end to it, in a way and as far as I was concerned, because we were then accompanying a singer instead of having a free time blowing. You had to be accompanying, which still had its own sense of fun, but it became less of an attraction. Then George took the band on the road, world tours, Australia, America, and again I couldn't do that.

You just fancied playing for fun?

Yeah. I was enormously fond of George. But musically I didn't see it as a step forward. And I didn't have the time either. I was just playing twice a week in pubs all within the London area. That suited me perfectly, it was tremendous fun. I played a lot with George and John Chilton. That was a good partnership.

So you knew George for years. What are some of your favourite memories nearer to the end of his life?

My favourite story... (Laughs) I mean towards the end George got slightly pompous. He did that Christmas gig every year at Ronnie Scott's, and then it changed hands and became less of a serious heavy jazz venue and it broadened itself up a bit. I saw him after he'd done the first one under the new management, and I asked him 'How was the new club?' he said, 'Oh it was terrible,' thinking that it was because the principals had all been changed, but he said, ' The doorman didn't know me.' So that upset him more than anything. And there was another occasion when the band and George played an old people's home. He turned up and there was a lovely old lady sitting at the front of the entrance. And she said 'Oh hello!' (very excitedly) and George said 'Oh, do you know who I am?' And she said 'No, but here comes matron, she'll tell you.' (Laughs)

That's a really good one.

Yeah. His ego tripped him up every now and then, but it was colossal and it took a lot to trip it up.

So you think he was kind of a loveable egomaniac?

Yeah! Who said that?

Me.

That's very good. But it was great fun doing the Flook strip. We spent a lot of time doing that together. He wrote the stories. We had a conference every week at the Daily Mail and we discussed future lines to explore. Then he filled it all out. He was more wordy than Humph, in fact it got to the stage when there was hardly any room in the frame at all to do any drawing. It was all balloons and words, you couldn't see the people. But we overcame that. You can't keep a good man down. But he had a huge success in later years as a singer. A lot of grey haired old ladies used to go along to be shocked by him. He got a lot of pleasure out of it.

Do you remember him more as a great figure than a musical talent? I think you once said he used to shout a bit too much.

Yes. The more he shouted the more out of tune it went. But some things he did were better when he took it more quietly. He was influenced by Bessie Smith mostly, and in those days they didn't have microphones. She used to sing down a great cone to get heard, to project the voice. Bessie opened it up and hollered away. Fantastic power. George did all that but with a microphone, not instead of. Without a microphone it might have been better.

So it was double amplified!

(Laughs) Yeah! He had such effervescence. I swore that I saw him smile out loud. It was all tremendous fun.

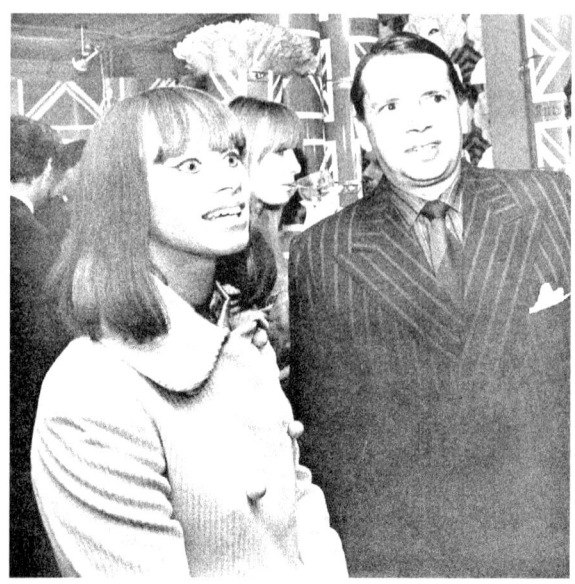

MELLY AS CULTURAL COMMENTATOR

"I met Diana in a bar," George later said about his first interactions with the woman who would become his wife until the end of his life. "My first wife Victoria was supposed to join me for the opening of The Establishment, but she couldn't come. She had fallen in love with a film director and phoned up the bar, where she'd knew I'd be, and told me that she couldn't make it. So I asked this girl I met in the bar, Diana, and she said yes. She was very beautiful. Afterwards we went up to Hampstead, where I was living, and made love on the heath immediately. Within a week, my first wife had left with the film director and Diana moved in; she and her two children."

George and Diana, with "two ready-mades" as Melly referred to her kids, were quickly married. They had a son, Tom, and breezed through the sixties as members of the swinging in crowd. This was sixties bohemia, and Melly was right in the centre of it as critic and cultural expert.

"I didn't give up singing," Melly writes in his Mellymobile book, "singing gave up on me." Indeed, Melly did not consciously jump ship, but a series of events occurred which led him into a totally different area. Adding to the amount of writing work coming his way, and the jazz scene losing much of it popularity, was the fact that George and Diana had the children to take care of, Tom and Diana's daughter and son from previous marriages, Candy and Patrick. The stay at home dad was writing for the Observer, reviewing music and films, and also doing some work for the BBC. He was a "personality" now, more recognisable to a wider audience than he ever had been while singing for Mick Mulligan.

Melly is one of those rare creatures, in fact one of the rarest of all. Not only was he a Surrealist jazz singer, he was also a man who made a living as a film critic for years, judging the work of others in print, and then having the guts and bravery to approach screenwriting for the cinema himself. Granted, Melly was a tremendously gifted writer who could make the most ordinary occurrence seem like some great Surrealistic illusion, but it was still a bold act to step up towards writing a film script. Sadly, arguably I might add, George never got to fulfil his cinematic potential in the two films he ended up having a hand in creating. That said, the fact he managed to script any film at all and see it filmed and released is miraculous. Still, one would love to have seen a Surrealistic Melly film come to fruition.

When Melly became arts critic for The Observer in the early 1960s, he was there to experience the cultural shift as, dare I say it, an observer and inside man. He wrote some fabulous pieces on music for the paper, but his film reviews were also brilliant, and it seems that with every film he reviewed his views were taken seriously and accepted as honourable and valid ones. Critical or not, Melly seemed to know what he was talking about when it came to art, music and the movies, in no particular order.

Some of my favourite reviews that Melly wrote for the Observer actually came in the early to mid 1970s when he was already re-starting his jazz career and just about to hand in his notice before going fully pro again. Melly has since commented that many films around this time were real clunkers, but the truth is he saw and wrote about some truly remarkable films, many of which changed the face of cinema, inadvertently or consciously.

I always gathered Melly would be a champion of Lindsay Anderson and his surreal style of poetic cinema, which somehow managed to be free of pretension but be visually and poetically inspired and beautiful at the same time. Anderson was a great art director but often regretted the fact he could not be anything but that, admiring directors like John Ford who could combine artistry with commercial success. Melly reviewed Anderson's O Lucky Man in 1973 upon its release, a cutting of which I have had for years in my scrapbooks of film memorabilia. Given that O Lucky Man is in my top five favourite films of all time, I find another area on which to totally agree with Melly. Clearly, I would have got on well with the man.

"There was every reason O Lucky Man! could have failed. It is picaresque, a word often used to excuse in adequate motivation. It is Brechtian, a mode which seldom works in cinema as the realism of the medium usually cancels out the alienation principle. The film works triumphantly. This is due in some part to the excellent multi role performances and to Malcolm McDowell's Candide like hero. But the film's success belongs to Lindsay Anderson. Satire demands a viewpoint and Anderson has one. The best British film for a long time."

Typically, Melly's real love in the world of cinema was the work of the legendary Spanish filmmaker Luis Bunuel. Luis had, of course, made the seminal Surrealist movie with Salvador Dali back in 1929, Un Chein Andalou, one which Melly and many others considered the truest and purest surreal movie. Melly adored Bunuel and all his work, even considering him the Greatest Filmmaker of the 20th Century. He admired the fact he dallied with Surrealism, but avoided bohemianism, remaining professional and approachable as both a man and artist.

Melly was open to all manner of film, however experimental and strange. The same year he praised O Lucky Man, he also reviewed the famous Warhol film Trash, clearly not shocked by this controversial new movie. "The film is a comedy, however black. The girl with the big boobs dancing and singing on her very own home vaudeville stage, the pimply Fritz the Cat-like schoolboy slumming for kicks, the mindless rich bitch and her despicable husband, Miss Woodlawn herself with her extraordinary tongue, an organ with an apparent life of its own, are really very funny. It may be possible to find Trash heartless, but to do so, I think, shows inattention. Every now and then, the camera settles on Joe's beautiful dead face and for a moment there flickers behind the eye a sense of pained, numbed outrage at what is happening to him. Once, a small tear runs down his cheek. These transvestites, nymphos, junkies are in hell. They frot and turn on to give them the illusion of living, the shadow of happiness. For all its superficial air of improvisation, this is a carefully considered, totally responsible film."

At the same time, Melly was not one to accept *anything* shocking that was put before him. Clearly it was about context, and in the work of British film director Ken Russell, Melly's penchant for the outrageous was challenged by this maverick's approach. He had been quietly outraged by his The Dance of the Seven Veils and called his even more shocking The Devils (1971) a "hymn to sadomasochism." George may have lived wild, loved the challenging world of Surrealism and was certainly known to let loose, quite explicitly in fact, at his jazz shows; but when it came to morals, he was not afraid to voice his views, and he had the pedestal on which to stand to do so. It so happens that his last days as a film reviewer coincided with the most controversial era in film history up to that point. Melly also wrote a letter to The Times to ban Sam Peckinpah's unarguably controversial Straw Dogs, released in 1971, due to what he saw as its immoral and graphic rape scene.

Melly's own brushes with film came much earlier when the movies were in the midst of its swinging sixties influence, and his work was much lighter than anything that Russell or Peckinpah could conjure up. Melly wrote the script for the 1967 film Smashing Time, directed by Desmond Davis and starring Rita Tushingham and Lynn Redgrave, not to mention Michael York. While other films depicting the sixties scene, perhaps the more supposedly serious ones, have aged terribly, Smashing Time looks very much ahead of its time in that it was spoofing, playfully I might add, the clichés and familiarities of Swinging London. Melly was clearly writing this, a man already into his forties, with his tongue firmly in his cheek. It's all so far out there and groovy that it just has to be a parody.

Though it did not set the box office alight and has been buried in the decades that have followed, it did attract some good reviews at the time of release. Roger Ebert, the legend himself, loved the film, even if he found Rita Tushingham's quirky looks off putting, in that he dreamt of proposing marriage to her throughout the film.

"Although the attempt to cover swinging London quickly becomes tiresome, there are several scenes so funny that they redeem the movie," he wrote. "Miss Tushingharn innocently begins a riot in a fish and chips shop, in which the weapons are spray cans of paint, shaving cream, deodorant and fertilizer. This is a preliminary to a really fine pie fight initiated by Miss Redgrave in a pie shop. A well-done pie fight is a work of art, and Davis knows the form well. There is the first pie, held in the hand as the idea of throwing it gradually occurs to the thrower. There is the moment at which the others on the scene decide to join. There is the impeccably dressed customer who is in the crossfire but apparently immune to thrown pies. There is the enraged owner of the shop. And there is, of course, the inevitable moment at which a window is open and pies fly out to hit (a) a clergyman and (b) a gentleman in a bowler hat. It is a very nice pie fight indeed."

"We thought as we were making it, this will be just right," Redgrave told Shawn Levy. "But the minute it came out people said, 'It's over. Swinging London is over'." Indeed, even by 67 the Swinging London idea was growing old, giving way to the "Summer of Love" clichés which dominate any retrospective cultural overview of the late 1960s. But Smashing Time is valid now as a kind of prototype Austin Powers slice of sixties spoofy camp, but remarkably one made in the era it is however consciously or unconsciously having a gentle laugh at. Even Michael York, here playing a Bailey-esque photographer, popped up in the later Mike Myers comedies as Powers' boss.

"Linnie and I, who had been friends since we were 18, absolutely loved doing it," Tushingham told the Guardian recently, "but nobody realised it was tongue-in-cheek - they thought we were trying to be trendy! Look at the scene at the end when they're at the party [for Yvonne's single] which everyone is trying to get into and be seen at. That's what it's like now. These days people really would go to the opening of an envelope, wouldn't they?"

Melly was happy with his first shot at screenwriting, though years later expressed dissatisfaction with his second script, for the 1970 film Take A Girl Like You, starring Oliver Reed and Hayley Mills. Again, it was a film which felt out of step by the time it was released, but might have been more relevant if released a couple of years earlier. Adapted from the novel by Kingsley Amis, and directed by none other than Jonathan Miller, it concerns Mills as a teacher and Oliver Reed as a dashing bohemian. For a while the film was a hard to find obscurity, but now it's readily available, even downloadable on You Tube of all places. Not as enjoyable as Smashing Time, but not as bad as some have made it out to be.

So Melly's dalliances with the film world were brief, and he exists more as an outside critic who dipped his toes in than an active participant. But the film work that is there, while not totally remarkable, is certainly worthy of your time and deserves a look if you are attempting to understand Melly's talents from every angle. Still, one cannot help but feel there was some potential untapped.

"What a great writer he was!" Melly's old friend Louisa Buck said to me on a recent phone conversation. That might seem like an obvious statement, but Melly's writing is so strong, so gripping and so witty that it inspires such simplistic praise. Perhaps it's because so much press, especially these days, focuses on Melly's personality, his bed hopping ways, his extravagant style, his hard living, and a little less so, his love of jazz. Surrealism is a word I link with Melly automatically in my mind, and it always has been, even when I was largely unaware of much of his output. But in the decades to come, Melly might just well be remembered most for his writing.

Melly was the writer for Trog's Flook creation, and wrote hundreds of pieces for the Observer, but for me his real essential writings are his books. Melly admitted he was no bibliophile, not at all, but he did have heroes in the world of literature and judging by the fluidity of his own text, must have read quite a lot of memoirs and autobiographical books.

Melly's first book was the legendary Owning Up, released in 1965, the midst of his writing career. Owning Up covers the legendary jazz era, from the late 1940s to the early 1960s when he hung up the jazz hat and put on the writing one (they were probably the same hat to be fair). It's a remarkable warts and all tale of a young man entering a world that would part-define him, almost by accident. His first meet up with Mick Mulligan is hilarious, while his adventures on the road would make Russ Meyer blush. In the end, you get the feeling that Melly wasn't too concerned with how his readers would take him, and he pulls no punches on himself, or his band mates for that matter. One of my personal favourite sections of the book is the final chapter, where he is thinking of leaving jazz and discovers his musical partner, Mulligan, is thinking of doing the same. He talks about what has happened to each band member rather romantically, as if to make a myth of the era he has spent the last couple of hundred pages exploring and entertaining us with. Owning Up is an essential read for anyone interested in jazz, though a fond interest in the genre is not at all essential in enjoying this book. If you love life, would like to learn a bit about it and send yourself back to a rustically magical era, then Owning Up is useful. One of the finest books about any sort

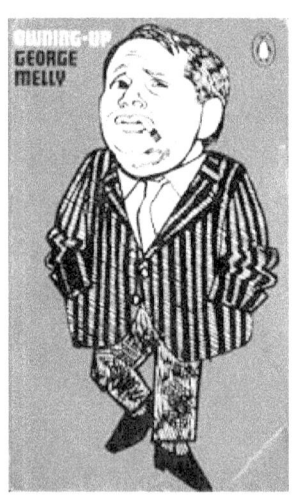

of musical activity, this is addictive reading and a perfect way in to the George Melly bibliography. Whatever the cultural mood, Melly seemed to be able to reflect it perfectly from every angle.

It's rather funny that he should have reflected back on an unfashionable music genre while covering the most current and popular one for a newspaper. George was definitely more associated with the pop cultural scene as it emerged into a serious art form in the sixties, and Melly as pop critic may have seemed like an odd possibility in the trad jazz days, indeed before pop took over all other musical forms, especially jazz, and began to dominate culture. But he was effortlessly brilliant in the field.

That said, he had more than a little help at home. "He knew nothing about pop music," his wife Diana said, "which I loved, so I was able to help him out." Diana also spoke about musicians coming to the house to be interviewed by George, such as Van Morrison, still with his 60s band Them, and other stars of the day. It's ironic that

Melly would start making a living writing about a musical phenomenon that killed his own jazz career, but his career was full of such contradictions and ironies right to the end. As proven in his seminal book Revolt Into Style though, Melly soon got to grips on this new boom, even putting The Beatles on the cover of it (or Peter Blake's artwork of them) despite having a brush or two with John Lennon, who once venomously verbally attacked him. "You jazzers," he spoke of Melly's contemporaries in derogatory terms.

When I visited her at home, Diana Melly said their life and marriage was at its most stable in the 60s when he was at home writing. "Things were pretty stable. Then he started singing again with Wally Fawkes and John Chilton, and wanted to get back out on the road." Alas it was not to be. It was the end of one chapter, but the beginning of a new one.

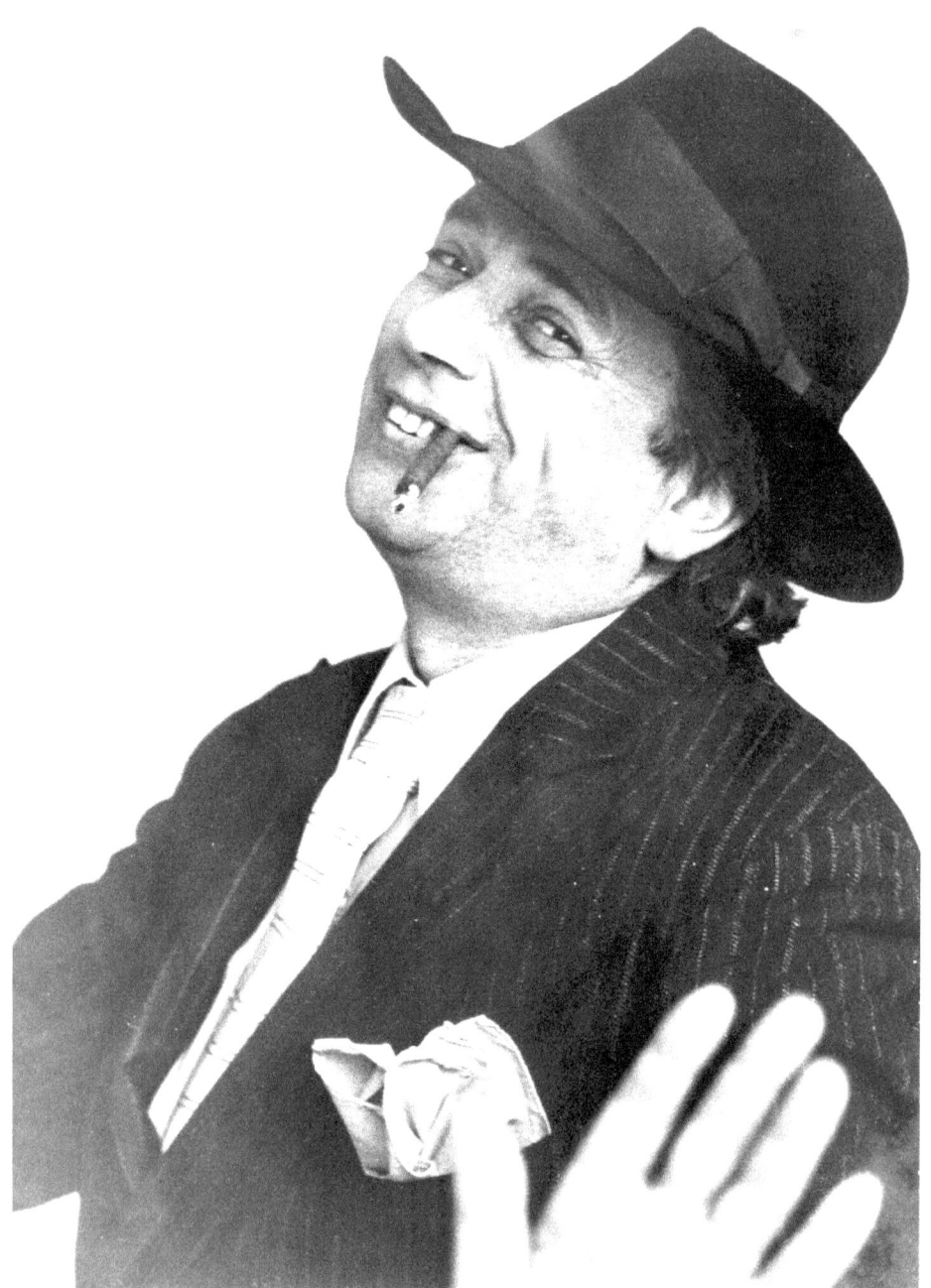

IN CONCERT

GEORGE MELLY
AND **THE FEETWARMERS**

WITH SPECIAL GUEST STAR

PETER SKELLERN

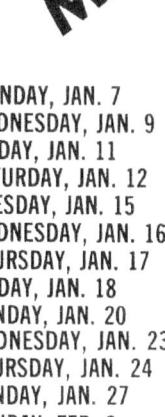

MELLY MANIA
74

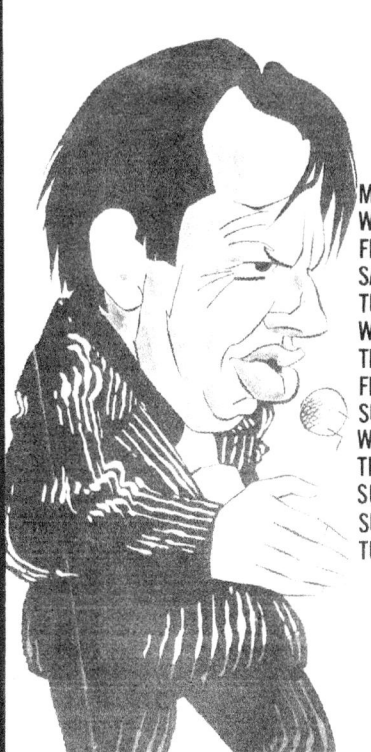

MONDAY, JAN. 7	BRIGHTON DOME
WEDNESDAY, JAN. 9	PORTSMOUTH GUILDHALL
FRIDAY, JAN. 11	BOURNEMOUTH WINTER GARDENS
SATURDAY, JAN. 12	BRISTOL COLSTON HALL
TUESDAY, JAN. 15	BIRMINGHAM TOWN HALL
WEDNESDAY, JAN. 16	SHEFFIELD CITY HALL
THURSDAY, JAN. 17	LEEDS TOWN HALL
FRIDAY, JAN. 18	SOUTHPORT FLORAL HALL
SUNDAY, JAN. 20	NEWCASTLE CITY HALL
WEDNESDAY, JAN. 23	EDINBURGH CALEY CINEMA
THURSDAY, JAN. 24	GLASGOW CITY HALL
SUNDAY, JAN. 27	FOLKESTONE LEASCLIFFE PAVILION
SUNDAY, FEB. 3	GUILDFORD CIVIC HALL
TUESDAY, FEB. 5	CROYDON FAIRFIELD HALL

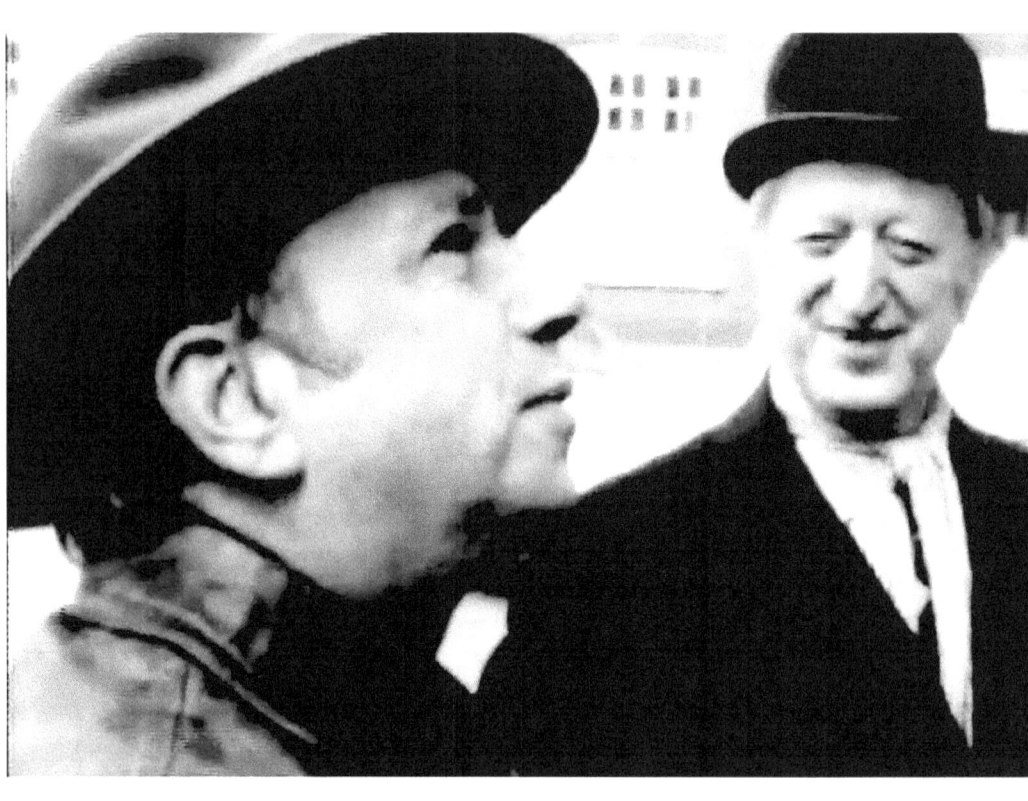

Melly observes a burnt out building in his surrealism documentary
for Arena, in 1978.

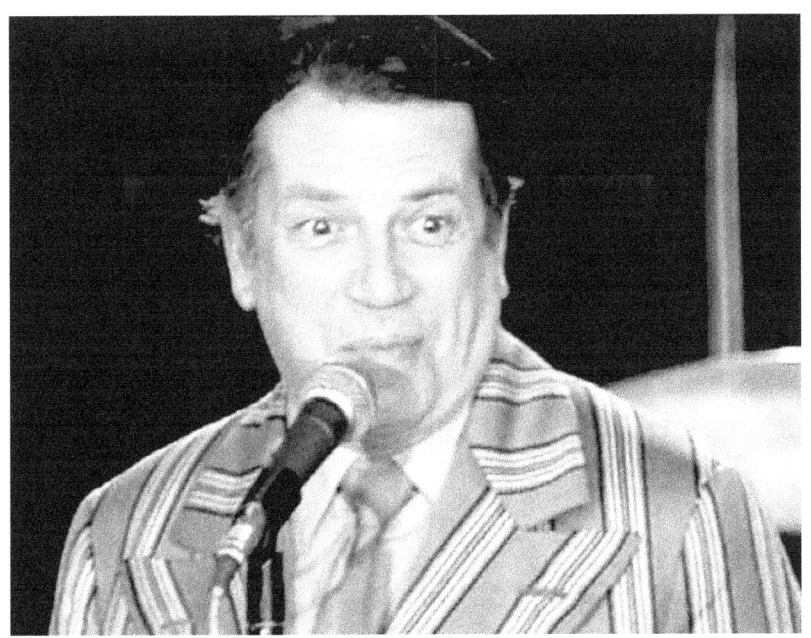

JAZZ, SURREALISM AND THE 1970s

By 1970, George Melly was in his mid forties, with a wife and children and various jobs that kept him very busy. He began the new decade with two pieces of non fiction, one of them a less celebrated one, a team up with cartoonist Barry Fantoni called The Media Mob, which directly profiled TV celebrities of the day and parodied the nation's obsession with these said personalities. Culturally, it was a spot on piece of social observation. But it makes one wonder, what would Melly think of our modern times, if he felt society placed celebs on too high a pedestal back in the early seventies?

"The Media Mob have invaded our living space," says the book, "and we have relinquished our territorial rights. The Mob are all household faces, your friends and mine, needing no introduction.

They are the aristocracy of the warm cod's eye, the cognoscenti of the idiot-box. The exact quality which transmogrifies a face into an icon is mysteriously arbitrary. It has nothing to do with talent or lack of it. Now Ena Sharples and Elsie Tanner are as much part of our mythology as Pickwick and Falstaff."

The last sentence seems to effortlessly summarise our obsession with fame, and by "our" I mean the world, not me personally. In an age dominated by Love Island, Big Brother and I'm A Celebrity Feed Me Some Kanagroo Testicles, this book which appears rather dated on the surface is almost like a wise and elongated Nostradamus prediction, a pre-echo of a total cultural breakdown. It is also a remarkable slice of contemporary social commentary, and though very of its era, it is ironically the book's near fifty-year age from which we can learn. If one were to be less cynical of course, the book is a harmless exploration of fame and the cuddly people who "invade" our homes and become known to us on first name terms alone. Alas, it seems more sinister and cynical.

One of the best parts of the book is Melly's assessment of Jimmy Saville, a monster of a man who fooled everyone for decades, even if quite a lot of folk were aware of some of his more sleazy and devious activities. If a man as smart as Melly was fooled though, Saville must surely be one of the craftiest and most depraved bastards that ever lived. "He doesn't really do anything, he just is," Melly writes of the fiend, then a "loveable" personality. "The mop of inappropriate dyed hair over the craggy, patently heterosexual face, the eccentric but meaningless clothes, the cigar, the parrot cries of 'Howzabout that, guys 'n girls?', the flat Yorkshire accent: none of it should add up and yet somehow it does. The reason, I believe is that (Jimmy) Saville is that rarest of all human creatures, genuinely good right through, a kind of bizarre saint. He's genuinely odd, too, with his big cars and his job as a hospital porter and his passion for physical endurance tests. But his goodness is manifest; people respond to it automatically."

Even Melly could be wrong it seems.

One of Melly's most acclaimed and still revered books is 1971's Revolt Into Style, an examination of pop cultural shifts in the 60s and early 70s. It could be said that along with Hunter Davies' less weighty Beatles biography of 1968, this was one of the first books to take a

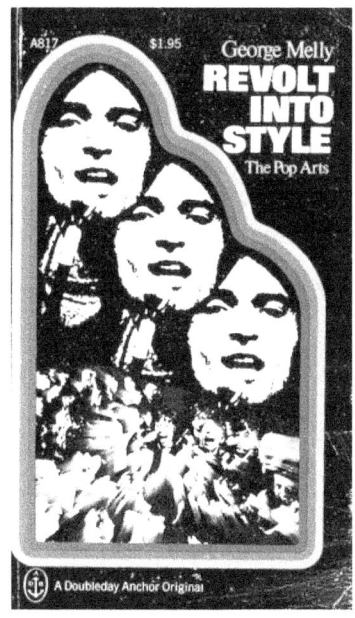

proper look at the importance and influence of pop culture. According to Julian Mitchell of the Guardian, it's the "first serious attempt" to do so, written essentially by a man who was part of it. And there is the secret to the success of the book. The text is not penned by some stiff dinosaur with countless qualifications and certificates on his wall, but a man from the school of life, a jazz singer and Surrealist who seemed to have an understanding of everything that was creative and worthwhile. Writing about art and culture for years at this point, Melly had become one of the cooler critics, a man who was considered to be an insider, on the side of the artists and in with them, as well as keeping one foot in the establishment. This is another reason Melly was a one off, in that he could fairly criticise work and do so with validity and still remain popular with the creative types.

Revolt Into Style remains one of the ultimate texts on the subject of pop culture, written over the latter part of the sixties and encompassing the all important Beatles (four fellow Scousers) in with everything else worthwhile in the era; film, literature, theatre, fashion etc. Melly comes across as informed and hip (though I hate to use the word), as well as being far removed enough from that revolutionary era to be able to commentate on it and observe its developments. (After all, he was born in the 1920s, weaned on jazz during the Second World War, and was two generations older than The Beatles.) What's really good about the book though is that it feels so exciting, mainly because Melly was writing it all as it was going on, not writing retrospectively when the decade was done and dusted and all the familiar clichés of the times were well developed. No, this is an authentic look at the pop art revolution as it happened, and it's probably in an exclusive list of one.

The book also explores the origins of pop culture, and sees how serious artists and figures in ages had adopted popular arts - like the Surrealists with the commercial medium of cinema, and writers like George Orwell. More interesting perhaps are the points raised about those looking down their noses at pop, like the jazz world and the folk purists, who viewed it with suspicion. Melly also considers the view that pop culture is the latest device in distracting and brainwashing the working classes. Again, many points he makes are relevant today. Like his Media Mob book, it highlights the emergence of a new popular icon, one replacing familiar icons of old that were beginning to slip from public consciousness and into the history books as the sixties drew to a close. It's an exciting book, and you'd be hard pressed to find a more essential text about that era.

As if to prove he was really was a highly fashionable member of the in crowd, though he did not do it for this reason, he was a witness at the infamous Oz Trials. Oz was a groundbreaking alternative newspaper/magazine which ran into trouble in the early seventies when it came under attack during an obscenity trial. Melly was proud to stand up in its defence. He was asked to take a stand and sum up the aims of the magazine and the alternative culture as a whole.

"The alternative society is one that tries to invent or evolve its own lifestyle, which is usually in opposition to the official lifestyle," he said in the court room, basically summing up his own view of life while defending the publication and the life style it promoted. "Oz is an organ which seeks to probe and to see what society is about. At forty five it's not for me the authoritative paper but I find it interesting and I learn from it, particularly about what younger people than myself are thinking."

Melly also said it was OK to use for letter words. When the judge asked him what the word "cunnilinctus" meant (clearly, he had lived a sheltered life), Melly educated him. "Sucking," he said. "Blowing. Or going down or gobbling. Or as we said in my naval days, 'Yodelling in the canyon.'" It was another classic Melly moment, but seemed to do little for Oz itself. Its last issue was published two years later, while the publishers were in 20 grand worth of debt. For George though, being attached to hip names like John Lennon and Yoko Ono, who joined in the Oz protest march, it proved he was fashionable and "with it".

George enjoyed his time as a cultural commentator in the 1960s, but even though he had a strong family life, nice house, good job, money, success, the right kind of fame and a generally steady going on, there was an itch that needed to be scratched. Only problem was, Melly didn't know what it was. At the end of 1960s, the mainstream music scene began to open up. The R and B boom of the mid sixties, which had put to death anything that wasn't beaten out by four or five hairy young lads with six strings, had lost its steam, and thanks to The Beatles and other mind expanding groups, more varied musical forms were acceptable once again in the mainstream. Even jazz, often a dirty word in the 1960s, was finding new popularity. George began making the odd appearance in the provinces and singing the odd song in London, not making money he says but just enough to cover expenses. He soon realised that this was the itch that needed scratching. "A performer is very similar to an alcoholic," George wrote, and one can see his point. He pined for the crowd once again, the musician's life style, the lure of the open road.

Melly admitted this desired return to the stage was ego driven, but the truth is that in the ten year gap since he had last been performing, his voice had taken on a whole new tone. Not only that, he was older, wiser perhaps, and singing those old jazz standards in a more weathered, world weary tone offered the material pathos, humour and genuine excitement. Melly had lived, no longer a snotty young lad, but a middle aged writer who found himself tempted enough by jazz to return, against all odds, to the dazzling (and often undazzling) world of show business.

At first, George began gigging with Alan Elsdon and his band, but he sought something more tight and reliable. Melly became interested in a band called The Chilton-Fawkes Feetwarmers who played every weekend at Merlin's Cave in King's Cross. They were a killer group, and George wanted in! He loved watching them at the "shabby" pub, where the landlord had split the bar and the live room in half so children could come into the venue, and drinkers could simply carry their pints in from the bar. It was a way of saving money, but as a result George said the atmosphere was grand, and obviously the audience was larger.

Wally Fawkes and John Chilton were up front in the band, as Melly described, blowing their respective instruments with passion (ooer!) and precision. Backing them up was a band including Bruce Turner on the sax, and Melly was tempted then convinced, upon request of course, to sing a few numbers with them. Melly felt a new excitement, with old chums returning to the scene, a buzz he'd not had since the 1950s.

"It was lovely to have some drinks, get high and sing with old friends," he said. "The audiences began to go cuckoo. The place became fashionable. We were asked to do concerts and to make a record. Suddenly, one day, I decided to take another crack at it. It had to do with the applause. It's like the alcoholic thing—applause is like the first fatal sip of sherry."

When George Melly seriously (though he was never that serious) returned to the jazz scene in 72, it was Derek Taylor who snapped him up quick and urged him and John Chilston's Feetwarmers to record and release an LP. Gigs had been coming more solidly, and Melly found that the thing missing from his life which he could not previously identify was that old mistress named jazz. With a fabulous band backing him up, and possibly the greatest music PR man in the world by his side, Melly set his sights on fame and mass adoration. Never physically vein by his own admission, he was hungry for the attention, and the best way to get people to look at him was when he was singing on the stage the jazz songs he knew and loved, injecting

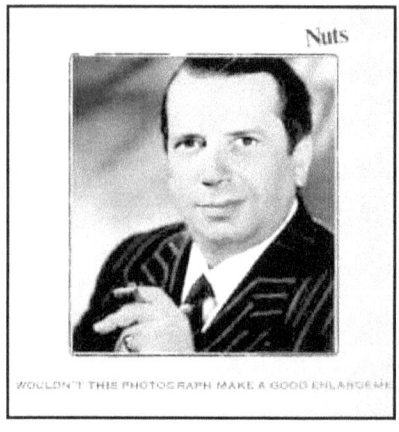

them with his characteristic individuality and his love of bawdy, good time thrills.

Melly and the band decided to record their first album together live at Ronnie Scott's Club in London. Typically, Melly didn't hold back during the performance and consumed a considerable amount of alcoholic beverages to aid him in his feral outbursts. A gathered crowd of friends - including Melly's very close chum Margaret Anne Du Cane, a countess - thoroughly enjoyed the night, as did Melly and the lads. The next morning however, Margaret advised Melly to listen back to the tapes before getting too excited about the record's release. When he did hear the tapes he was horrified, though also amused, by a rather less than polished vocal performance. The booze was clear in his voice, and it was evident in the general musicianship of the band too. The whole thing, save a few numbers, was in George's words, "an escalating shambles."

"There were hundreds of people at Ronnie's when we recorded Nuts and some very outré behaviour," Melly recalls, going on to describe women undressing and unleashing their inner beasts. "Everybody was terribly drunk, including, alas, us. At the end, I went raving up to a girlfriend of mine who was sober and said, `Wasn't that great?' and she said, `Wait until you hear it in the morning'."

Though the recording was a wreck, Melly and the boys did impress Ronnie enough for him to hire the group for a week, and continued to do so for years, often at Christmas for a festive night of lewd fun ("Here's George Melly," Ronnie used to say, announcing him from the stage, before adding, "God help us all!") and bawdy thrills. With the recorded cuts not being up to scratch, the band and Taylor went into a recording studio in South London to lay down some new renditions. Famously, they ran up an expense bill that consisted of 87 bottles of wine and fish and chips for the whole gang.

As well as its frantic recording, the cover art for Nuts has also gone into Melly folk lore. According to George, Taylor took him to a professional photographer down Oxford Street to get a nice snap of him for the cover. "They airbrushed out every line" Melly recalled, "and hand tinted the resultant bland visage which in consequence resembled the work of an American mortician."

George Melly may have looked reserved and respectful on the album cover, but on the contents of the record he was anything but. In fact, he was more wild and feral than ever before, while holding it all together with effortless cool. One of George's friends, Louisa Buck, spoke to me recently and summed George up as a man who was both out of control but also in control at all times. The Nuts album seems to prove that theory. The recording was done in a studio, but the added audience sounds from the other recording lend it a certain authenticity, while George's charismatic performance keeps a certain level of excitement up at all time, not to mention an atmosphere of camp naughtiness that is very much of its era.

Mapledene Car Hire
LIMOUSINES and SALOONS

Head Office
280 Queensbridge Road
Hackney E8

Transport Office
Fernsbury Street
London W.C.1

м NEW MERLINS CAVE
MARGERY ST CLERKENWELL WC1   19

TO WEA
FOR THE ATTENTION OF
MR DERIK TAYLOR

To Food Supplied in the Hall FOR Guests		150	-	-
To FISH & CHIPS DINNER ETC		16	-	-
To WINE				
87 BOTTLES GIANT SIZE				
2 LITRES AT £2·75		239	25	-
16 BOTTLES 1 at £1 50		24	-	
57 BOTTLES at £1 -		57	-	
TO BEERS				
1 18 GALLON KEG AT 20 pence		28	80	-
1 " " BITTER 20 "		28	80	-
1 " " LAGER 24ᴾ Pint		34	56	
TO DRINKS SOLD OVER THE BAR		26	30	

TO MR GEORGE MELLY called
FOR By HIS MANAGER. THE SOUND
ENGINEERS and MR TAYLOR
AND HIS GUESTS AND STAFF
WHO ALSO HAD DRINKS WITH
THERE DINNER

THE HALL		100	-	-
2 REHEARSALS AND THE RECORDING				
Please pay - Derek Taylor. TOTAL		704	71	

The album is full of crisply recorded, wonderfully played Melly gems, to which the great man brings his effortless charm and relatable approachability. Anyone put off by the J word must learn that there are all types of sub genres within that large encompassing genre, and Melly's music sits on the authentic but accessible border. Indeed, Nuts is an album even a jazz hater might enjoy. The musicianship is, of course, flawless, with the band on top form. Chilton's colourful trumpet, always complimenting Melly's vocals, is continuously solid throughout, and the arrangements by Chilton himself are tastefully well observed.

His take on the old classic Dr Jazz is a striking cut, with Melly's voice at its most fun and care free, while their rendition of T'Ain't Nobody's Business is fabulous and among the best here. The band swing nice and cool, while Melly holds back a little and stays faithful to the song. He holds the band with his deep tones.

The title track is simply wonderful too, among his most well known numbers and a definite crowd pleaser. Swerving double entendres or subtle innuendo all together, Melly goes all out and enjoys himself shamelessly, unapologetically. One wouldn't think that hearing a middle aged man say "he plays with his nuts every night in bed" would continue to please you after countless listens, but for some reason it does. This is Good Time Melly magic. "I hate Nuts," Diana Melly told me with a smile. "How many times can you hear about a man playing with his nuts?" My answer is a lot.

Elsewhere there are more sombre and bluesy cuts, like a wonderful version of Nobody Knows You When You're Down and Out, which Melly gives real depth and weight. Sugar is so smooth it almost hurts, with Melly's vocals more restrained and giving way to a beautiful arrangement. Viper Mad, the energetic closer, is simply marvellous, featuring some great solos and a wound up and rather wild Melly vocal. As a stand alone record, outside the folk lore of Mellydom, Nuts is of its time but also timeless, like all good trad jazz music truly is, and is an all round solid album in its own right. Melly's risqué lyrics and fun loving crooning style might jar with the ears of some modern listeners more used to polished, clean pop and PC lyricism, but for me he gets it right. These are solid interpretations, and some 46 years on from its recording it remains a rich and endlessly enjoyable LP, one which gets spun quite often in my domicile. More music should be like this - unashamedly fun and a little naughty to boot.

The Guardian gave it a glowing review during its 2004 CD reissue. "Everyone should have a George Melly CD in the house, for those moments when life gets a bit too solemn, and this is the one to have. It features the original Feetwarmers, with Wally Fawkes (also formerly of this paper) on clarinet and Bruce Turner on alto saxophone, both playing beautifully, as does trumpeter John Chilton. George excels himself, especially in the title song, a masterpiece of single entendre."

Anyone reluctant to dip their toe into Melly waters, perhaps put off by sniffy, snobby critics who turn their noses up at his habit of making jazz light and full of humour, might want to take on Nuts, because even though it does feature trademark Mellyisms and harmless Carry On style smut, the musicianship is staggering and undeniably good. You never know, even if you're a full time Melly doubter you might find your foot-a-tappin' to this record.

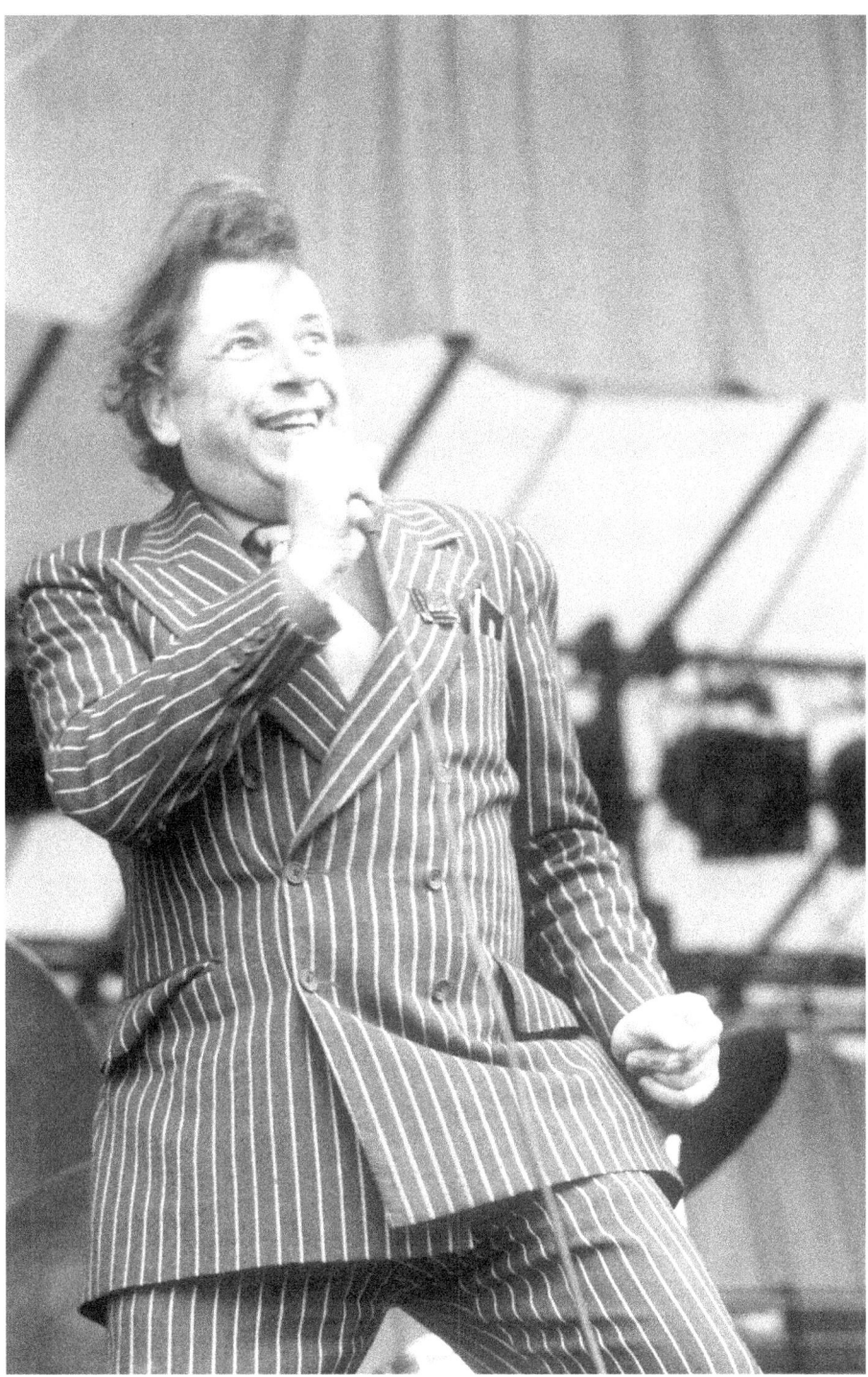

It was after the relative success of Nuts that Melly and Chilton decided to go at it again full time, and they began to gig furiously for the rest of the decade and beyond. In his book Mellymobile, he recounts the joy of looking at the log book and seeing every single date, give or take one or two, filled with bookings. In the same book he recounts all kinds of interesting experiences; memorable nights at The 100 Club for instance, where he used to play back in the old days (he recalls some toilet graffiti which says "George Melly is A Puff", under which someone has written, "Worse still, he likes girls!"); meeting fans and admirers who are often over keen and expecting him to dive straight into bed with him, regardless of sex or looks; going back to Liverpool and having a wild night out with his uncle, who slopes off blind drunk halfway through this particularly hedonistic outing; heated arguments with shoddy hotel staff; trips to New York for gigs, staying in Little Italy amidst the colourful Italian American characters etc. etc. While Melly and Mulligan's days in the 1950s often get the attention for being the great legendary time for George Melly the Jazz Singing Star, the seventies more than live up to those sepia tinged days of old.

Only a year later, Melly and the Feetwarmers returned again for the sequel to their smash Nuts LP. Son of Nuts was a more rowdy affair which didn't even try to hide its wild, appealing bawdiness on the sleeve. The cover itself, featuring a far less polished image of Melly on stage singing and looking, it has to be said, slightly demonic, was like a prototype Derek and Clive sleeve, with its sleazy newspaper cuttings and harsh photography style. Indeed, the picture is much more fitting and appropriate than the clean cut George of Nuts. Cover art aside the album itself is just as nicely played and recorded as its predecessor. There is a slightly different vibe, a subtle difference in the general atmosphere (perhaps Son of Nuts seems more real and raw), but in many ways it's Nuts Part 2.

It opens with the rather apt greeting from George himself, "Hello Decadence", before the full band come swinging in to a tidy version of Old Fashioned Love. The mood is low and easy, while George's voice is superb, the atmosphere chilled. He perves things up a notch with the highly sexually charged I Need A Little Sugar In My Bowl, in which he delivers a mighty awe inspiring performance; his deep, rich voice giving the recording genuine atmosphere. But one can tell he is also deriving a lot of pleasure from singing the thinly veiled double entendres. Yet the rudeness doesn't cheapen the whole thing somehow. The music, so sweet and strictly tasteful, masks the sexual element behind its delicate organisation, and Melly knows when to step aside for the band. Yet the mischievousness is there, evident beneath the sleek surface.

There are even lighter moments on the LP too, such as a genuinely funny and eccentric Show Me the Way to Go Home, which Melly lends some peculiar magic all of his own. In the liner notes he says it was not included for musical reasons, but to prove that everyone did indeed get very pissed. Good Time George, a signature song for the legendary partier, is tremendous and impossible to resist, swinging along beautifully with Melly up front declaring his reluctance to miss a chance to rave. He's up and down the country, this relentless hell raiser, taking his music to the people. But he warns fathers and husbands to lock up the girls, because George is out on the prowl looking for fun. While these days such a statement would probably garner police attention, back in the 1970s this was good harmless fun. Ah, to bring back those nostalgic pre-PC dominated days.

Heebie Jeebies is another mini classic too, with Melly's vocals as smooth as they can be, effortlessly gliding through the tidily 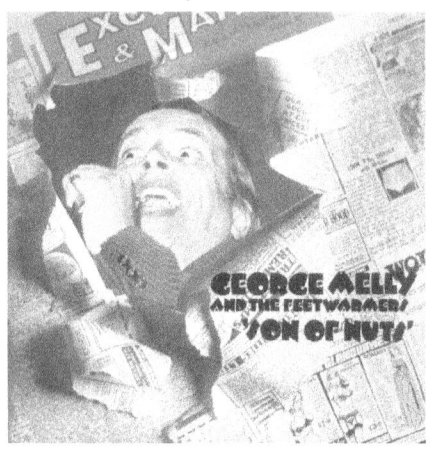 arranged standard. Kitchen Man, another one he recorded back in the old days with Mulligan (and would record much later with Digby Fairweather in the new millennium), is given a gorgeous treatment, with some splendid playing from Fawkes on clarinet, Chilton on trumpet and Colin Bates on the piano. Melly though, sounds like he's been transported from another time and place, and it's a vocal effort which sends shivers down the spine. His voice is not technically perfect, of course, and he works within a framework which works for him, but there is a power, an insatiable enthusiasm and genuine class that really does send you off to another plain all together. On songs like these, one can sit and appreciate the sheer passion Melly had when performing before an appreciative audience. So authentic it stings, this is Melly at his best.

Son of Nuts was another winner for Melly, both critically and commercially. That said, it's hard to find many bad notices about Melly at all. Indeed, he seems to be one of the few figures who drew warmth and affection from almost everyone who knew him, or even just knew *of* him. If anyone was unaware of George and they needed a direction, now he is gone, towards an album that captures his glory in this golden era, then undoubtedly you'd have to send them towards Nuts and Son of Nuts, two glorious records which have stood the test of time. Though they were reissued together on a great double set in 2004, it's time they saw another release on CD, perhaps as separate entities, and maybe with outtakes and rarities. (How about the scrapped first recording session, eh? Now that would be a blast to hear!)

Seeing as Melly was still making a living from the odd spot of writing too, he had to be careful what venom came forth from his pen. "I wrote once that Birmingham was the arsehole of England," he said. "I thought I'll never go there anyway. Then I went back on the road and the first gig was in Birmingham. I was a bit apprehensive. When I got there, people came up saying 'What did you say... that Birmingham was the arsehole of England?' I said 'It's probably all changed now.' And they said 'Oh no, it still is!'"

Melly grew wilder and more flamboyant as the decade went on. As he went from success to bigger success, behind closed doors he and Diana's marriage became officially open and he began to enjoy a series of varied affairs over the next few decades, while still being married to Diana who provided the foundations of his heady life style. There were all kinds of women, from artists and lorry drivers to writers and countesses. There at home though, without fail, was Diana.

One of these women was the artist Elda Abramson. They met in Manchester after a gig and found they had a shared love for jazz and Surrealism. They soon became lovers, but speaking today Elda prefers to think back to their rich and rewarding friendship. "He was such a kind man," she told me, recounting a time when she had tax problems and to solve the issue George hired out a hall, gave a speech on Surrealism and gave the proceeds to Elda to pay the bill. "All you read about is the bed hopping," Elda said, frustrated that the press's idea of Melly is as a sexaholic booze hound.

As the gigs continued to come thick and fast, so did the albums. After Son of Nuts, It's George followed a year later in 1974, and it was another gem. Its release coincided with Melly appearing on the TV performing songs from the record on Bernard Manning's legendary Wheeltappers show. Melly was at the height of his fame and popularity.

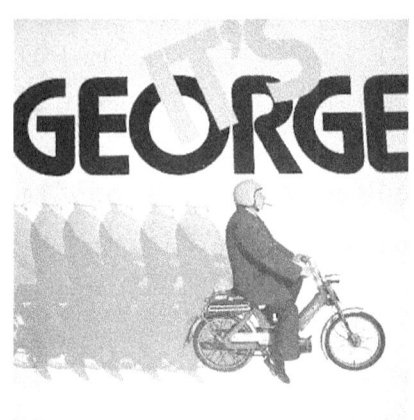

The band on It's George are fabulous; Chilton is reliable and brilliant as ever, constantly complimenting Melly's voice with well timed passages and superb arrangements; Chuck Smith, again, reliably enough, is fabulous on the drums; Steve Fagg's double bass is incredibly rich and deep; while Colin Bates' work on the piano remains one of the record's strongest musical elements.

That said, even considering how spectacular the music so often is, Melly remains the star throughout, a man made for the central role in every way. Granted, without the accompaniment and essential presence of Chilton, the album would be nothing musically, but George is the one to pull you in and keep you hooked from start to finish.

The band tear through the standards like they are taking no prisoners; It Don't Mean A Thing is a fabulous opener, while the originals are just as fun and rewarding, like Chilton's own Give Her A Little Drop More. Perhaps the best known and loved song on the LP is Boogie Woogie Man, which along with Good Time George, became one of his trademark cuts. It's guilt free fun from beginning to end. The album version has a terrific drive to it, but I can't help but admit the live version on Manning's show is far superior in terms of energy and Melly magic.

Not quite up there with the essential and fresh Nuts and Son Of Nuts (which admittedly are hard to beat and have a certain freshness to them, considering they were Melly's first recorded work since his ten year hiatus) but It's George is a great little record in every way. The sad thing is, like many of Melly's 70s albums (and some of the 80s ones too) it has never been released on CD. Thankfully, obtaining a second hand vinyl copy is fairly easy these days, and chances are it will be signed too. And who can resist that front cover, with Melly on a moped complete with ciggy in gob. Classic.

Funnily enough, in the midst of his musical activities, Melly made another return to film in the mid 1970s, not as a writer, but as an actor. In 1974 he had a small role as a director in the plain bonkers but addictively viewable Sweet Movie, directed by the controversial Yugoslavian filmmaker Dusan Makavejev. Dusan was renowned for his earlier film, WR: Mysteries of the Organism, which Melly later interviewed him about (you can watch the fascinating exchange on You Tube folks!), but in some ways Sweet Movie is more arresting, and certainly more outrageous too, which is definitely saying something. Sweet Movie follows two women in two separate narratives. The first involves Miss Canada winning the prize of marrying a milk tycoon, and this is where her trouble starts. The other follows Anna who is on a sweet filled boat in Amsterdam, who ends up stabbing her lover to death and tempts children into her boat, in a bid to convert them to communism, by luring them with candy. It really is mad, and the kind of film one might expect, in

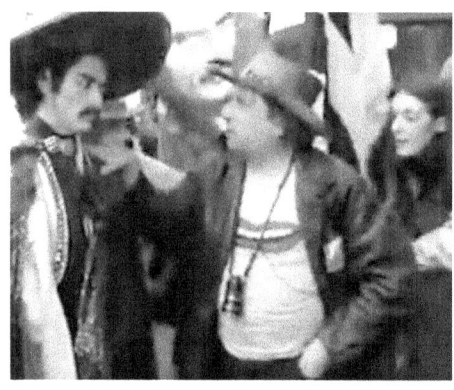

theory at least, to come from the pen of George Melly. His scene as the cowboy hatted director is brief, but extremely enjoyable all the same.

The New York Times were rather unimpressed by the clear excessive extravagance of the film, which is personally one of the things I liked about it. "As Mr. Makavejev has brilliantly demonstrated in his earlier films — particularly Man Is Not a Bird —he can make films of comparatively conventional form if he wants to. Now he obviously doesn't want to. This independence of spirit is laudable, but when it involves the large amounts of money that apparently went into Sweet Movie, it begins to seem decadent. Too much money is being spent for the benefit of the few. When Miss Prucanl and Mr. Clementi make love in a bed full of sugar, one forgets the metaphor and starts to worry about how they got all that sticky stuff off after the scene was shot. On two occasions male actors urinate onscreen, once in a close ‑ up. Is this real or were of devices used? When the audience begins to wonder how an effect was achieved instead of why it has been done, a film's claim to seriousness flies out the window. Earthquake and The Towering Inferno made no such claims. Sweet Movie does—and fails."

At this stage, recording albums and touring the UK was just a part of the Melly life. While writing on the side and partaking in his favourite activities (raving and fishing pretty much), he was forever in and out of the studio with his band, when the touring schedule permitted it of course. Melly Is At It Again emerged in 1976, released on Reprise, and featuring a camp picture of Melly in full dandy get up. The line up added Ray Russell on guitars and production was handed over to Geoffrey Haslam. Derek Taylor, who had guided Melly and company so well in the early seventies, was out of the picture now, meaning that one vital piece of the Melly entourage had moved on. Still, even without his presence, Chilton and Melly are a formidable and perhaps unbeatable duo when it comes to bringing the standards of the old days up to modern times.

Takes on Jelly Roll Morton songs like Milenberg Joys and Animule Ball are good if slightly unremarkable given Melly's usual high standards, but Jeepers Creepers is pure gold, as is the faithful When My Ship Comes In. Melly is At It Again doesn't just rely on the oldies though. The album also contains a couple of original tracks by Chilton himself, like the brilliant Punch and Judy, and a nice reworking by Melly and Chilton of Marie Laveau.

For me though, they leave the best until last. Pennies From Heaven, the album's closer, was also pulled off as a single, and Melly lends the very familiar song some genuine warmth. Such is Melly's charm, he can refresh, update and totally reinterpret a familiar song and completely make it his own. It's almost as if some of these old songs were written just for him.

Melly Is At It Again is definitely not among his finest works, but then again is not his worst either - not that he actually has a bad album mind you - and doesn't contain a single dud. Wonderfully played and worked out, it's another reliable record that is easy to find on vinyl but still lacking a CD or download release.

Melly was an established icon in the UK, but in the late 1970s he was also getting a bit of a following on the other side of the pond. In 1978 he found himself with a residency at Michael's Pub in New York, the venue where Woody Allen and his Jazz Band were and still are regulars. On the 2nd of June in 1978, a write up of Melly and Chilton's show appeared in the New York Times which praised Melly and his band to the skies. They dubbed him "The Englishman Who Sings Like Bessie Smith" and raved about his showmanship and vocal skill:

"There is usually something incongruous about a white man trying to sing a black blues. Even more incongruous would be a white Englishman's singing the classic black blues associated with such women as Bessie Smith and Ma Rainey. But a 52 year old Liverpudlian manages to bridge this awesome gap three times a night at Michael's Pub. He is George Melly, who is also an authority on Surrealism, the writer of a successful comic strip, a television, film and pop music critic and the author of three books, including a study of the origins of the pop music of the 60's. Not to make it any easier for himself, Mr. Melly performs in a purple shirt, white tie, tan and black plaid suit and a huge black hat that makes him look like a cross between a character from Guys and Dolls, a caricature of an old style

Southern senator and, with his round, mobile face and startled eyes, a huge, eager frog."

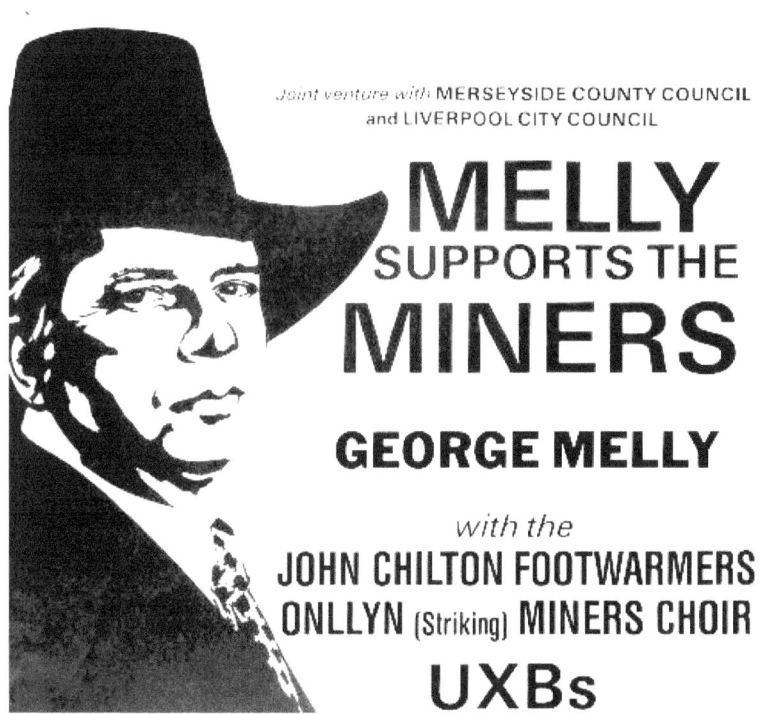

Joint venture with MERSEYSIDE COUNTY COUNCIL and LIVERPOOL CITY COUNCIL

MELLY
SUPPORTS THE
MINERS

GEORGE MELLY

with the
JOHN CHILTON FOOTWARMERS
ONLLYN (Striking) **MINERS CHOIR**
UXBs

Melly's previous performance in New York, this one at the Bottom Line in 1974, had received some harsh criticism in the Times. Melly himself said the writer was getting his own back because he'd previously made - quite rightly he claimed - minor criticisms about this particular writer's work. A score needed to be settled, rather unfairly it must be added. He dubbed Melly "a squat, leering figure of androgynous sexuality, a stylistically frivolous performer of camp vaudeville." Harsher critics of Melly were sniffy that he put so much lewd fun into jazz, and were also sceptical that a white middle class

Englishman should want to sing like a black person. Melly though, couldn't have cared less.

"But the criticism has come from earnest, young, white critics," Melly said at the time his act started going down better in the Big Apple. "I have instant rapport with black artists. Jimmy Rushing was a dear friend. Roy Eldridge likes what I do. When I met Carrie Smith at Ronnie Scott's in London recently, she said. 'He may look white but he isn't.' How can I talk in an English accent and sing in a black voice without embarrassing myself or other people? Well, if I were a Welsh tenor singing Italian opera, nobody would say you can't sing in Italian. Once, I sang St. Louis Blues in an English accent. It was ridiculous. Besides, I tend to sing songs sung by theatrical performers, not primitives. I'm not pretending to be sitting on the porch of a shack in Georgia with a guitar."

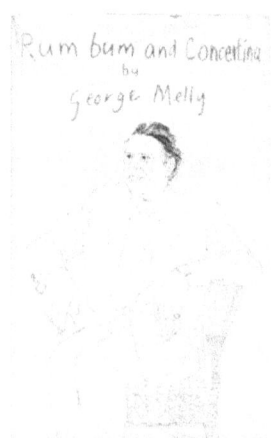

In the midst of all this, there was the release of his notorious naval based memoir, Rum, Bum and Concertina. The book that made Melly a firm gay icon, despite the fact he wrote it in 1977 when totally straight and already wed to Diana for 15 or so years, Rum, Bum and Concertina sees Melly exploring his life whilst in the navy. Colourful and outrageous, it recounts Melly's then love for the chaps. The late Richard Smith summed it up nicely when he wrote "It was published in 1977, when it was still rare to hear a man write with such relish about a penchant for bum." Definitely the most risqué and salacious of the memoirs (though they all have their moments, to be fair),

Melly does not hold back for one minute and does not try to hide from his gay past from behind (ooer and all that) his consistent if often troubled marriage. No, quite the opposite. Melly is proud of those man loving days and it is from such books that society could look to see that liberation and acceptance of homosexuality - or in Melly's case, bisexuality - is not a new thing. Again, George was light years ahead of the rest, and definitely a forerunner in regards to sexuality and how open one wants to be about it. Honest, raw, and hilarious, another book that's hard to put down once you start reading.

George Melly's career was full of all kinds of unexpected and exciting twists and turns. The way he could juggle being a jazz singer, a serious Surrealist, a raver, a fisherman, a sophisticated art critic, a womaniser and a family man was extraordinary in itself, but his life was full of occurrences that may have even caught the open minded Melly by surprise. One of his most memorable encounters came when he met a certain bunch of angry upstarts in 1978. Ever one to encourage younger people in various creative fields, Melly recorded a song with The Stranglers, one of the most successful and exciting of the punk and new wave groups to emerge at that time.

He first met the band (consisting of Hugh Cornwell on vocals and guitar, JJ Burnel on bass, Jet Black on drums and Dave Greenfield on keyboards) when he was working for the BBC on a special about Dada and Surrealism. When being asked if he could think of anyone form modern contemporary culture that had carried on the spirit of Dadaism, Melly mentioned The Stranglers and invited them on to the show. In a remarkable moment of the documentary, Melly heads towards the gallery where the exhibition on Surrealism and Dada is taking place, and walks down a very interesting alley adorned with posters advertising the current city activities of the day. He drifts by The Stranglers, who stand on the street corner, pulling faces and hamming it up like good Dadaists. "Long live The Stranglers," Melly says before leaving them to their strange existence.

Melly and the boys must have got on well, for before he knew it they had invited him round to the studio to work on a song. Hugh had written the lyrics for a track called Old Codger especially for him ("I don't know what they were thinking," Melly said in 2000, "I'm not much of an Old Codger now!"), all about a priest enjoying inappropriate activities with the choir boys. On the resulting recording, a punchy blues rocker, Melly gives it some real juice and an air of sleazy glory, even adding in ad libs like "Just close your eyes baby and think of England!" and, perhaps best of all, "Ah why do I always keep my socks on?"

Hugh Cornwell later said that though he disagreed with Melly's idea that The Stranglers were Dadaists (I side with Melly on this one, as the man definitely knew his art) he was excited to record with him all the same. Before the session commenced, he met Melly by the river early in the morning to find him lying on a park bench with a bottle of whiskey in his hand. Upon a handshake and a swig they headed to the studio.

"George turned up with a tin," Cornwell recalled, "and he gave it to me because I'd said 'Do you mind if we roll a joint?' 'If you're gonna roll a joint, you might as well use some of that. It's rather good.' He brought out this tin and inside was this huge fucking lump of very, very strong hashish. So I thought Good ol' George! He was a bit of a wild man too..."

Around a decade ago I spoke to the late record producer Martin Rushent, who recalled working with The Stranglers and George Melly on the Old Codger song, which was to be used for the B side of their next single, a cover of the Burt Bacharach song Walk On By. Also joining Melly in the studio was a chap called Lew Lewis, a harmonica player with a fondness for drink.

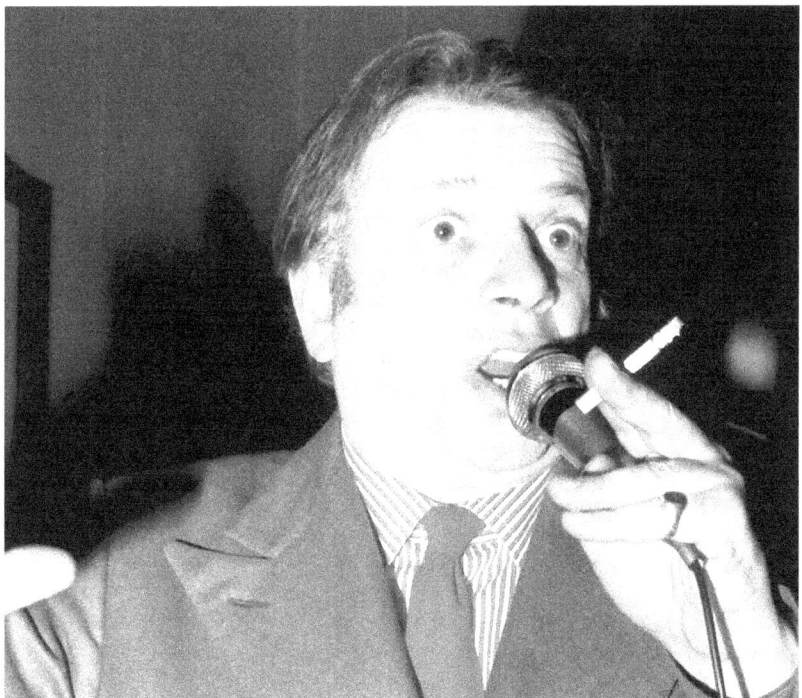

"We had Lew Lewis in; he was a fun guy," Rushent told me. "Lew turned up to do his session on the harmonica for the song. We had George Melly in too. Now George Melly was a brilliant guy; just the most likable person and he was great fun to work with. I think he was wondering what the hell he was doing there sometimes. Anyway, he (Melly) did his thing and it was fucking brilliant. Then Lew Lewis did his harmonica part and then proceeded to get very drunk on Jack Daniels. He had bought a couple of bottles in and started to neck them when he'd done his bit and we were working on something else. He went outside to the shed that was used as sort of a rest room at TW Studios, and he came from that shed downstairs and straight into the control room door. I'm sitting there and suddenly Lew comes through horizontally about 4 feet off the floor. My memory of it is he seemed to come in horizontally and then drop like he was flying. He was so drunk that he completely missed the step and had fallen forward."

The song itself remains a personal favourite Melly moment on record. Though definitely not jazz, and not very surreal for that matter either, it does capture some of Melly's more off the wall qualities. It's utterly mad and wild, with a charismatic, lived-in, throaty and hilarious vocal performance.

Melly had another brush with The Stranglers after this, when they put him in their seldom seen music video for Walk On By. In it, Melly and a Dionne Warwick lookalike walk around a park and generally piss about while being followed by the lad who played harmonica on Old Codger, Lew Lewis. Hugh directed the arty short. "It was all right," Melly recalled. "It was a nice day and I'm very fond of Hugh. He asked me to do it and I said sure. I haven't seen it yet. I knew it was a skit of Blow Up, and it was filmed in the same location. I spent two days just walking backwards and forwards with this very beautiful girl."

Stranger things have happened of course, but there aren't many, if any in fact, old fifties trad jazzers who would be considered hip and cool enough to team up with a punk band at the height of the movement and come away looking cooler than the supposed punks themselves.

But Melly had his own music career to focus on. It's strange how one album can be simply so-so and another can be a stone cold classic. It's especially weird when it's from the same artist, and features most of the same people and kind of material. But it's true that some LPs simply have a sense of magic about them; they glow and radiate a certain fifth element which is hard to define. There are a few of these type of LPs in George's discography for sure, even though he puts the same level of commitment into his whole catalogue.

One of the best records Melly released in the 1970s, or in his whole career for that matter, was Melly Sings Hoagy (1978), recorded for Ronnie Scott's record label and featuring the Feetwarmers and other chums. Again, only available on vinyl (someone get a CD out, please!) this one is also very easy to pick up, and I have to say it's well worth doing so.

The music being fabulous (obviously), it's also interesting to read Chilton's notes on the back of the sleeve. A jazz expert in his own right, and a very fine and acclaimed writer on the genre, Chilton finds it fascinating that composer Hoagy Carmichael and Melly's lives have so many unlikely parallels. "Each of them benefited from a private education," he wrote, "Neither of them originally intended on becoming professionally involved in music. Both were extremely recalcitrant young servicemen who later became involved in the film world - Melly as a writer, Hoagy as an actor..."

The piece goes on to explain that both men's lives truly began when they heard jazz and were awakened in a way. Chilton also recalls showing Melly a Hoagy song made famous by Louis Armstrong, but when he showed the Hoagy recording to him he instantly fell in love with it. "When George got into the booth," writes Chilton, "he could hardly wait to get into the studio to begin recording. Most of the songs were ones he had known since his teen age days in Liverpool."

The enthusiasm shines through brightly, and it's the passion evident on this recording which more than likely elevates it above some of his other records. The opening Riverboat Shuffle sets the mood of classy arrangements, flawless performances and whole hearted, impassioned vocals, but songs like Lyin' to Myself scale even bigger heights. Rockin' Chair, a Melly favourite he would play right to the end, is here in its definitive form, a beautiful version with an excellent vocal performance. The music, too, is sublime. Melly is clearly having a ball with the melodies on Lazy River, where he really channels the groove and soul of the song and takes himself off into a new area of eerie and spiritual authenticity. The Nearness of You is also flawless, the music arranged by Arthur Greenslade lending itself fabulously to Melly's tones.

Side two begins with the more jaunty Hong Kong Blues, going on to the glossy Lazy Bones, another one featuring an effortless and charming vocal from Melly. One of the finest on the record though has Melly going deep down there on New Orleans, possibly the most velvety performance, and the purest take on Hoagy's music he does on the whole record. It might be obvious to state, but Melly spookily embodies a twenties New Orleans black jazzer so well that it's slightly unsettling. If you didn't have the sleeve with Melly's face on it in your hand it could be most puzzling.

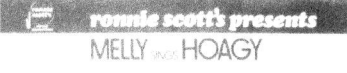

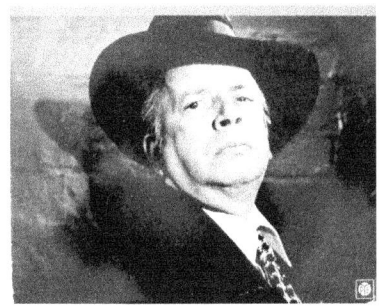

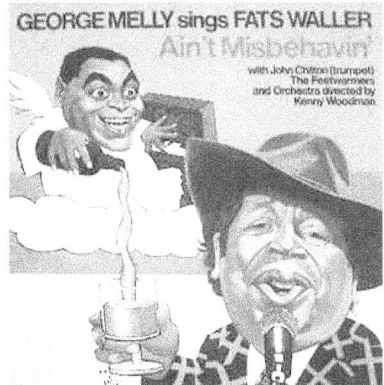

More polished than the previous albums in some ways, it's largely the production by Terry Brown which brings out the best in the music. The performances are all sharp too, and George in particular shines brightly, sounding totally in control of every single note he lets escape, almost spiritually, from his mouth. For my money, it is definitely one of his best recorded albums, unjustly underrated and sidelined.

Melly juggled jazz with his other passion in life, Surrealism. George Melly was, for many people, the ultimate British Surrealist of the 20th century, despite not contributing any actual art to the movement, at least not publicly. Despite this, he was perhaps the most pure of Surrealists, for he lived the surreal life from the beginning to the end, long before he knew the meaning of the word and long after it was a sizeable, serious concern. "I still fly the flag" he said as a failing old man, as the increasingly few loyal Surrealists limped on with their bones-a-creaking. Louisa Buck, his one time girlfriend and fellow Surrealist crusader, said he definitely kept Surrealism alive, and was ever keen to pass on his love of the art form, spreading wisdom to new disciples with genuine love and affection for the aims outlined by Andre Breton over a century ago.

In an excellent film made in the late 1970s with Alan Yentob for the BBC Arena series, George made some valid points about Surrealism, and what people so often misunderstand about it. The fact they are making the same misassumptions today proves that Melly's words made sense. Many people use the word "surreal" as a neat way to define something strange, wacky and bizarre, something mystical perhaps or so off the wall it makes no sense. To Melly though, Surrealism was defined on a basic level, in one way at least, by getting something ordinary and combining it with something ill fitting to create a new way of looking at the entity in question, making the ordinary extra ordinary, or at least viewing it as so. Mysticism and Surrealism may seem to be separated by a thin line, but in fact Surrealism is all about embracing the absurd which is actually around us but often unseen to most, while mysticism promotes fantastical imagery. Surrealism is a feel, a vibe, an atmosphere.

"Surrealism is not an art movement," he said in the documentary. "It's a way of life." If Surrealism really was and is a way of life, then Melly certainly lived a surreal life in every way. As the artist Giorgio De Chirico said, one must live in the world "as if in an immense museum of strangeness." George Melly certainly saw the world through a Surrealistic prism, this is evident in his writing (especially in Mellymobile, a collection of his Punch music travel articles, where minute details become Surrealistic snap shots; not to mention his seminal Paris and the Surrealists essay book) and sometimes in his music performances, though they admittedly veer towards Dadaism.

Melly lived out his days, until the very end in fact, as a Surrealist. In a more recent documentary on Surrealism for Yentob's BBC series Imagine, Melly, by then ill and frail, quoted his friend, the artist E.L.T. Mesens, who had uttered these immortal lines on his death bed - "I am a surrealist to the tips of my finger nails!" These had been Mesens' last words, but this was a mantra Melly himself adopted and lived out with loyalty.

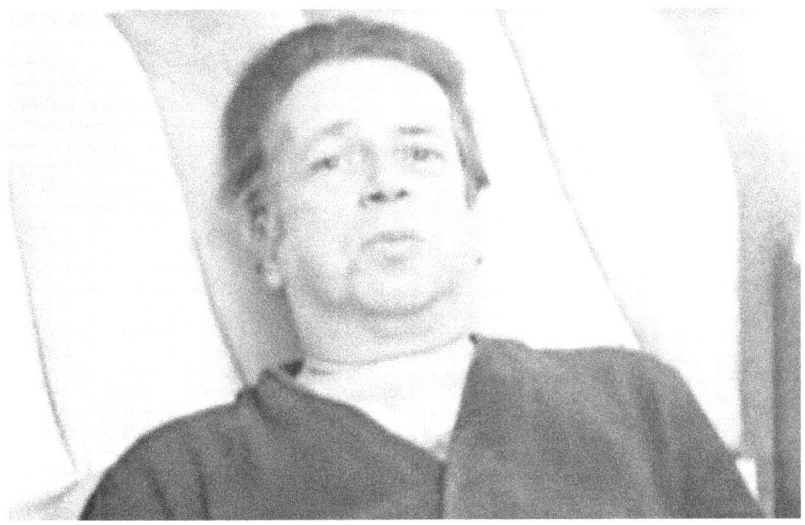

And were there links between jazz and Surrealism? Melly thought so, but only a little. "There's a little bit in that jazz is an improvised music and that automatism entered into certain areas of Surrealism," he told the BBC. "Yes, the Surrealists were social rebels, on a very deep level they wanted to liberate human beings from the prisons they like to be in. But Surrealism for me was not simply a school of painting but an attempt to point a way to a greater freedom in which the conscious and unconscious would be considered equals, in which light and day were equal, dream and reality equal."

The Arena episode featuring Melly remains a firm classic, and anyone not a Surrealist convert should maybe take 30 minutes to view this, and maybe wonder why you've been overlooking Surrealism for so long.

He may have been praising the less accessible world of Surrealism in the late seventies, as ever, but he was also promoting the more straight forward medium of jazz too. George Melly Sings Fats Waller, released in 1979, is another gem and among my favourite of his recordings, mainly for its sense of no frills loyalty to the music it is paying tribute to. If Melly had annoyed his harshest critics by singing black songs in a black voice, he didn't take those criticisms to heart, nor did he care what they had to say about his voice in any way. Taking on the music of Fats Waller was as big a statement as he could have come out with in light of such criticisms. But George knew all too well his vocals fit Waller's material, and that of many of the old black legends of America, and that he could offer something new to their work while staying true to it. "In America," he said in 1978, "people who have heard me on record, not all that many I must say, think that I am black, which is very nice, because this is what I hoped I would sound like."

The record itself is well worth the price of purchase, although sadly, again, it's not out there on CD, just original vinyl. Melly tears through, quite brilliantly in fact, classic songs like Squeeze Me, a particularly brilliant Ain't Misbehavin', the excellent Your Feets Too Big and Honeysuckle Rose. It's when you hear Melly interpreting Waller that you realise, alongside Bessie Smith and perhaps the "soul" of Louis Armstrong, how many voices and styles he managed to often unconsciously include in his own true voice. Somehow, this "Jewish middle class Liverpudlian" was able to get the same feeling out of these old songs as the original artists did. Was he tortured? No. Was he black? No. Was he poor? No. He was none of these. But Melly still had the feel for the music because it was in his roots, and his love and devotion to these songs went back to his early life. "Jazz was a marvellous antithesis to suburban Liverpool life," he said, something he could equally have said about his love of Surrealism.

Melly enjoyed a fruitful if bizarre decade in the 1970s; near pop stardom, a hook up with a new musical partner, a seminal book on the pop arts, a team up with a punk rock band, several brilliant records, a best selling naval memoir, and even a film appearance in the plain unsettling but hugely enjoyable Sweet Movie (1974). In many ways, it was his most interesting era, and for me at least, his most fascinating. But then again, each Melly decade is full of wonder and memorable incidents.

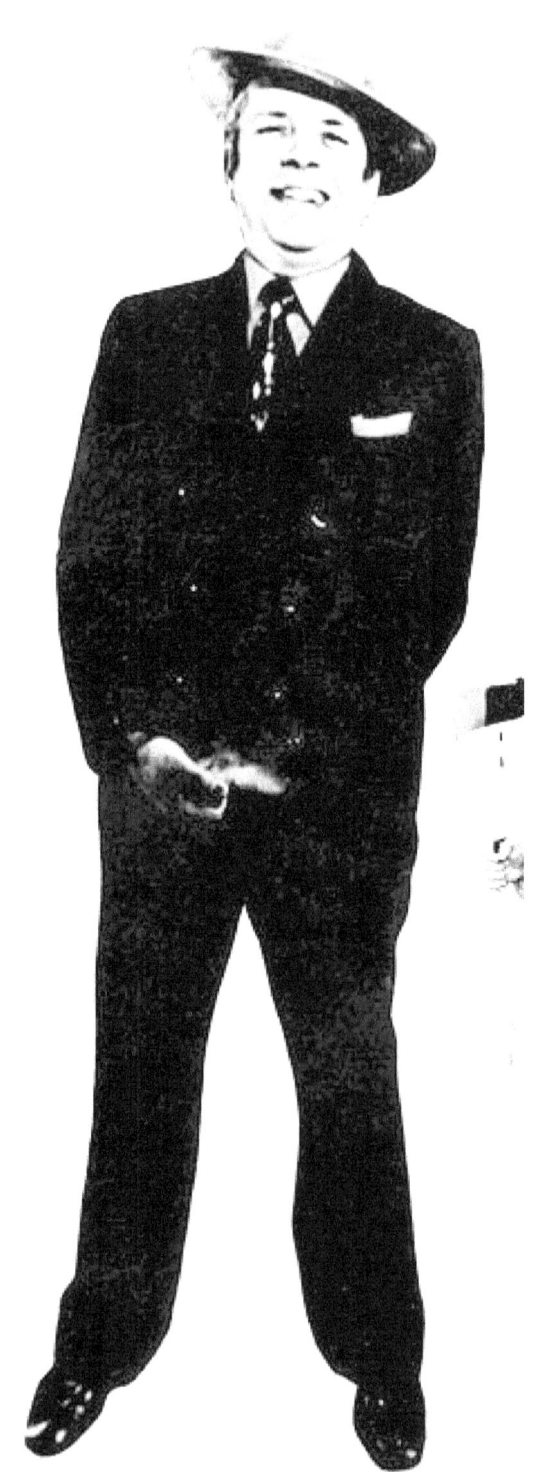

Corby Festival 75

Late Night Shows

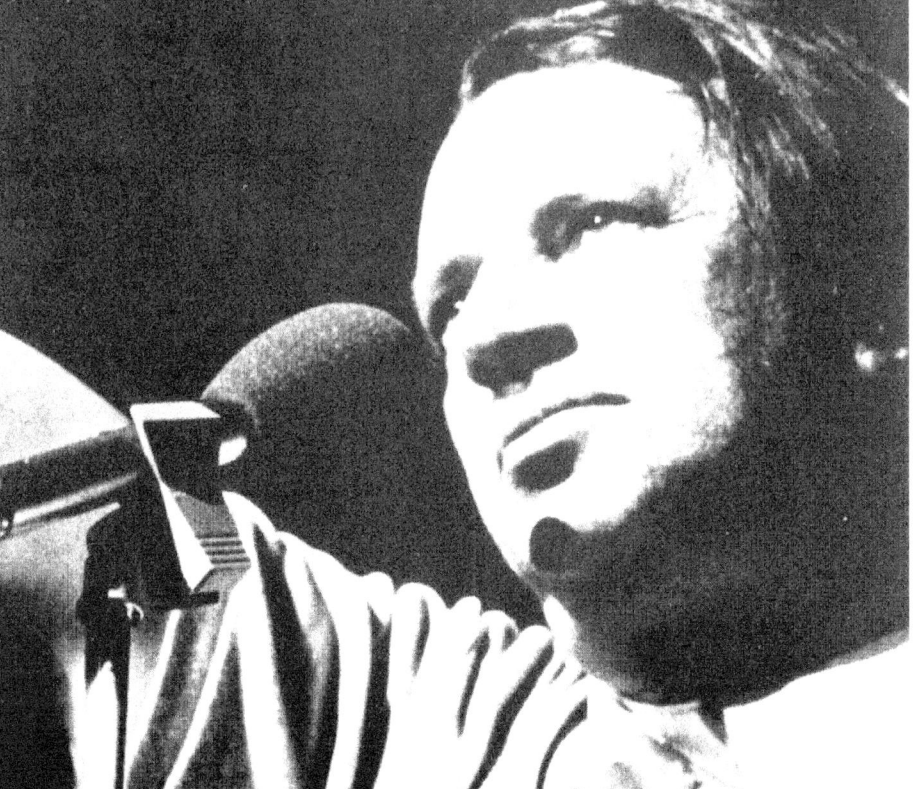

GEORGE MELLY

Melody Maker

DECEMBER 29, 1973   9p weekly   USA 50 cents

...AND A VERY MELLY 1974!

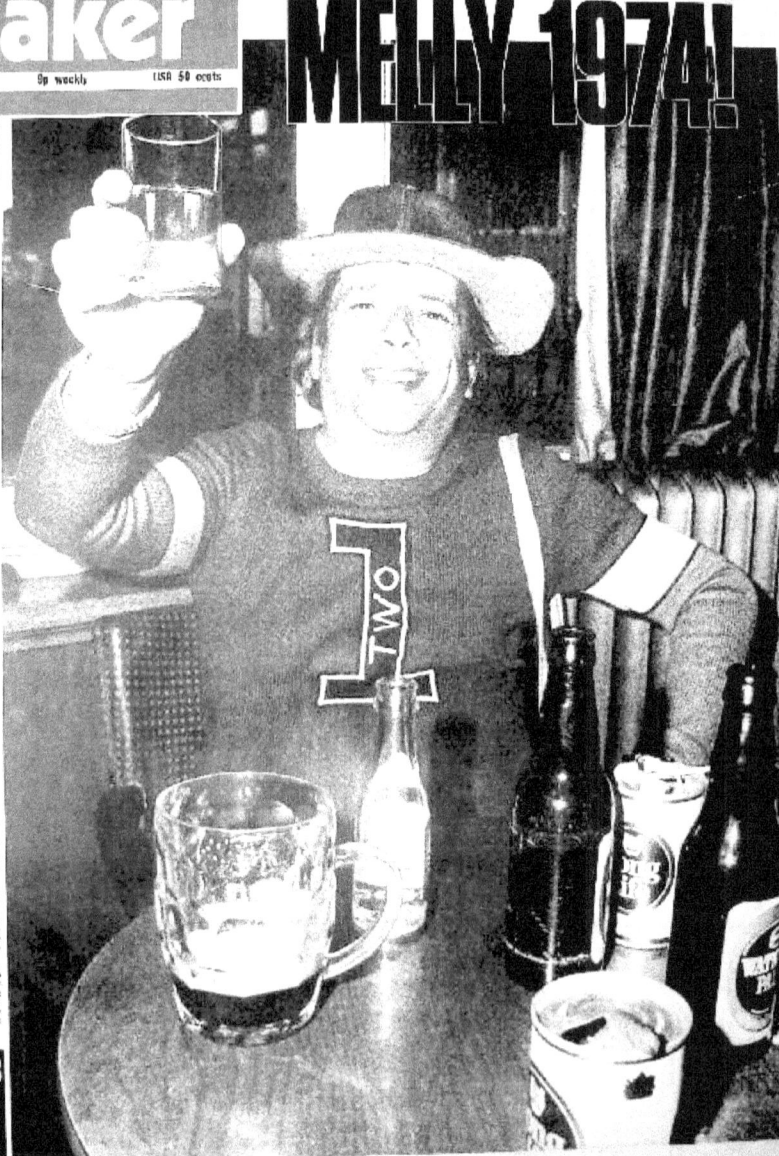

GEORGE MELLY hits the road next month — sponsored by the Melody Maker.

It will be George's first major solo tour — marking his return to full-time professional gigs. Georgie scooped the Male Singer Award in MM's 1973 Jazz Poll.

The tour, presented by Pete Burton in association with MM and the Peter John Chiltern Promotions, plus special guest star Peter Skidge.

And, tying in with the tour George will be on BBC TV when he has already started on "The series of six programmes for Saturday viewing, starts early in January.

The tour opens at the Brighton Dome on January 4.

The full sched will include a full house plus George singing with the entertainers.

Following the opening at Brighton comes Ashford at Croydon, Surrey the dates are the same for Croydon, Bournemouth (11), Cardiff, City Hall (Feb 11), Leeds Town Hall, Birmingham (15), City Hall, Manchester (17), Town Hall, Leeds (19), Free Hall, Southport (20), City Hall, Newcastle (22), Sheffield City Hall (23), the City Hall, Glasgow (25), Dundee to Paisley, Edinburgh (27), Free Hall Glasgow includes (1) and further halls, Croydon (1).

Full details for the tour are planned at all dates which will be forthcoming from the promoters. Tickets prices details are available at each venue's ticket office.

Dylan delay

BOB DYLAN'S new album, Landscape, still has no release date in Britain — because there isn't a label. Asylum have signed Bob to a worldwide deal in this country.

Dylan's label is distributed in the States by Asylum, which has signed the first release Joni Mitchell album is due for American release next month to coincide with Dylan and the Band's U.S. tour.

But soon to hit before he leaves, to be connected with the Band. He has to discuss before they hit the label — although a release date and MM this week that a decision was expected at any moment.

Goodbye '73 Hello 1974
SURVEYS INSIDE

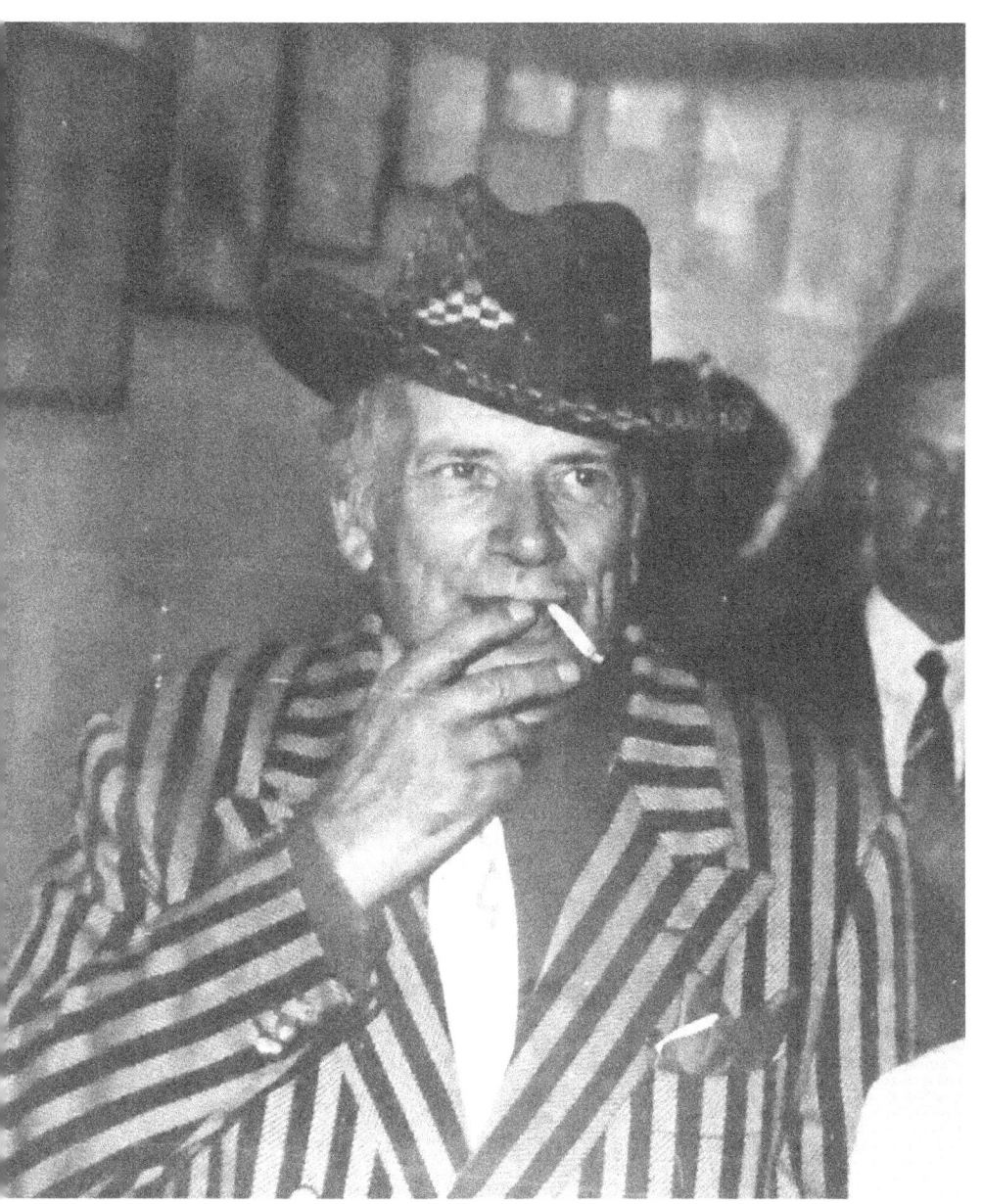

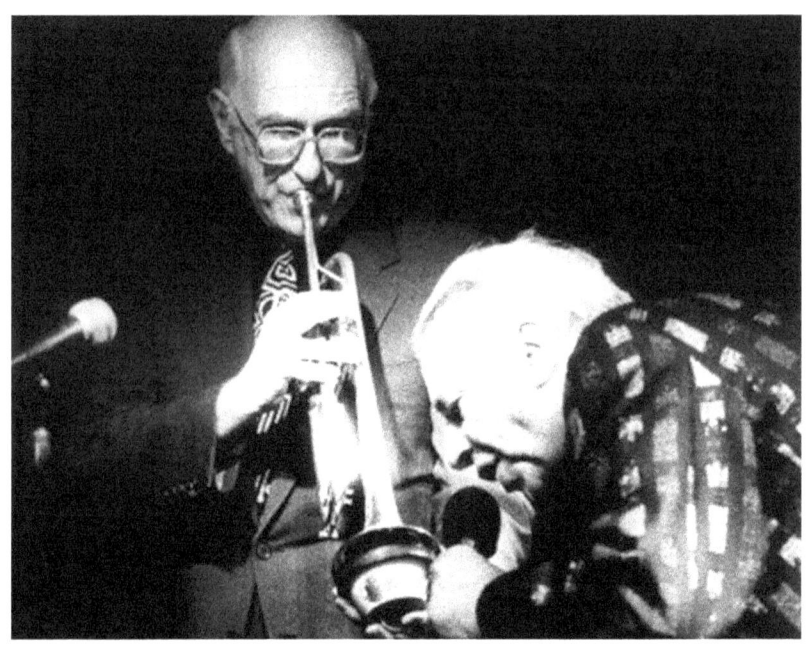

A JUGGLING ACT: THE 80s AND 90s

There were a few things which remained constancies in George Melly's life; women, booze, fishing, Surrealism, his wife Diana, and of course, his jazz. For George, it was just a question of juggling them together. "He devoured everything," Louisa Buck says of this man who had so much enthusiasm for art and life.

As the 1970s turned into the 1980s, Melly and John Chilton continued with their career as lauded and highly popular jazz entertainers. Melly stuck to what he did best, singing in that raunchy, exuberant, enthusiastic style, with Chilton as his right hand man, trumpeter and arranger. As the years went on, Melly found the job got easier, but no less fun. As he carried on playing clubs and the university circuit, Melly was pleasantly surprised to learn that modern audiences were more open minded.

"Now I work with John Chilton I have extended what I do," Melly said with confidence in 1983. "I would never have done a Cole Porter song in the 1950s. Now there are certain ballads I enjoy singing, although the centre is still the sort of jazz I sang 40 years ago. 40 bloody years ago!"

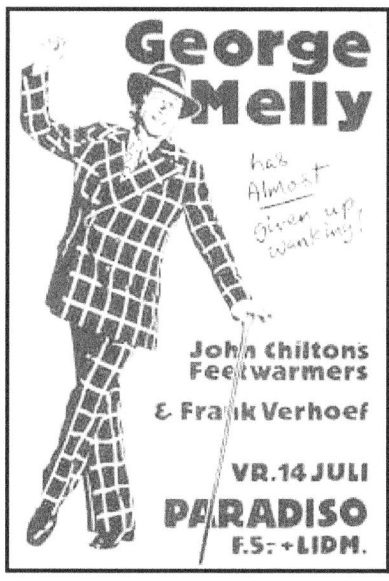

One might think that someone so associated with the swinging sixties and the saucy seventies might have felt out of place in the Thatcher led 1980s, an era of ever advancing technological innovations and "greed is good" ambition. But the truth is, Melly found the decade more open if anything, especially compared to the sixties. "In a way I feel more comfortable now for the simple reason that in the 60s anyone over the age of about 26 (or 36 certainly, which I was) was considered senile and rather disgraceful. This is now not the case. I have relationships now with young people which are very easy. There aren't all those barriers, like the refusal to use words, that people had in the 60s. You see I rather like talking. There are good things that are happening now: there is less of that exclusion of general culture, of the idea that an old master has to be boring or that a nineteenth century novelist has to be rubbish. There's a wider sense of what's acceptable. There's a lot of one's contemporaries coming out in search of their wild youth. But there are also a lot of young people coming and listening to us, especially in universities and technical colleges which we wouldn't have set foot in around 1965. Now we play a wide variety of jobs: everything from Oxford May Balls, to technical colleges, jazz clubs, theatres, but mostly concerts. And the audiences are mixed age groups — up to 60 but down to 17."

The 1980s were an equally strong period for George Melly, even if he didn't quite reach the commercial heights he had in the 70s. His first LP of the new decade was Let's Do It in 1980, a glorious affair complete with a rather camp album cover featuring Melly hamming it up on the phone, evidently taking part in a conversation on the sleazier side and feigning shock at the lewdness. (It reminds me of the earlier 10cc record, How Dare You?) It's trademark Melly fare.

The music itself is glorious. Gonna Catch You With Your Britches Down is a terrific opener, setting the mood perfectly for what is to follow. Though you'd think no one could inject new life into an old number like Cole Porter's Let's Do It, remarkably so Melly does just that with his ballsy rendition. His voice, which he now has an admirable control over, is effortlessly cool, bringing out the simplicity of the melody but adding a dose of cheeky charm. Again, Chilton's trumpet compliments him, always a step behind, shadowing his full yet controlled vocals. The band play superbly too (a fine band at that, consisting of Chuck Smith on drums, Barry Dillon on bass, Stan Grieg on piano), but Melly's appealing voice holds it together in many ways.

Elsewhere, Chilton, Melly and company perform true and loyal versions of such old classics as Bessie Smith's Backwater Blues (a

Melly favourite, he'd later duet on it with Van Morrison), and the bawdy gem, which was often a live Melly favourite in the old days, I

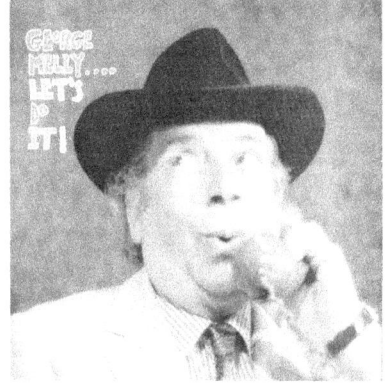

Want My Fanny Brown, as filthy a song George could sing - and that's saying something!

Other tracks on Let's Do It sound as if they were written for him, and indeed, Melly does make them his own, effortlessly it seems, on what is one of his most fun and abandoned records. Was I Drunk is a buried bit of gold, while hearing Melly's take on Downhearted Blues feels like an essential listening experience. It closes with On Revival Day, a seamless end to the record.

Let's Do It is a solid set, full of strong material and decent performances, but it's one you'll have to be content to own on vinyl only. Let's face it, there ain't going to be a George Melly reissue campaign any time soon. But perhaps that isn't so bad after all. Personally I feel Melly's music works better on vinyl anyway, and there's something much nice about lifting the needle on to the record, watching it spin, and hearing Melly's voice, crackling ever so slightly, echoing across the room, as if alive and sat beside you.

Other activities may have quenched George's thirst for discovery - his TV work, art criticism, other writing, chat show appearances etc. - but at the end of the day he was first and foremost a jazz singer. He'd spent ten or so years away from the stage, but when he stepped back upon it in front of those bright lights and adoring fans, it was a drug he couldn't quit, even to his dying day.

One of the most entertaining and fun Melly books is the collection of columns he wrote for Punch magazine, Mellymobile. The editor Alan Coren, who employed him to pen these light, informative and engaging entries, also suggested the idea for the book, and calling it Mellymobile seems to be the most fitting title. The book begins with some details from George about how he ended up back on the road with John Chilton and the Feetwarmers, tempted to the mainstream recording world by Derek Taylor, and then goes on to the columns themselves. There are all kinds of wonderful adventures here; Middlesbrough becomes a Surrealistic place of minute detail, his uncle gets blathered and has to return home, Melly rocks the 100 Club, meets old fans who can't believe he's jazzing again, comes across two brothers who look nothing like because their mum was friendly with the milkman (Melly also notes neither of them looked like their mother or father) and makes his name in New York. This book has been long out of print now, but can be obtained in second hand form for an almost insultingly low price. Buy it, but be warned, it will probably be impossible for you to put it down and may be read in one sitting.

Melly's books usually appeared sporadically, but in the early 1980s three popped up together in one year. A great doorway into a whole sub category of Melly myth is the 1981 book A Tribe of One, which explores various UK naive painters. Never snobbish about his art (a rarity within art critic circles I'm sure), Melly was never one to look down his nose at something, especially if it had aesthetic value as well as intellectual worth. In this book, Melly explores the often overlooked world of more primitive styles. Gorgeously illustrated, the only real fault is in the fact it's such a brief read. But then, with works by such greats as Scottie Wilson and James Lloyd, not to mention Melly's eloquent, classy text, it's a fascinating mini study that still feels complete despite its briefness. For further information on Melly's interest in primitive and unusual art, track down his 1994 documentary about Dakar, where our man journeys to Africa to look at primitive art from every angle, some of them rather unexpected and others very impressive. (He meets some interesting characters for sure, and even drags up for a hilarious dance off with the locals.) Also worth a look is the Artisan Pictures documentary, Outsider Art, which features Melly visiting an outsider artist chum and offering his views on the art, calling one artist's work, familiarly, "for a tribe of one."

A minor and very short Melly book (under 50 pages actually) 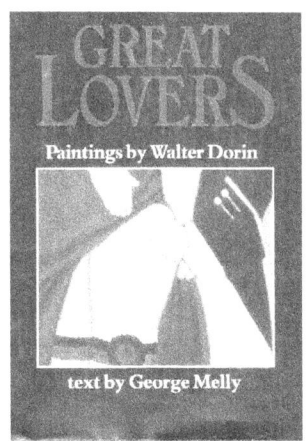 consisting of text by George and artwork by Walter Dorin was Great Lovers. The point of the book is to depict the romances of the title, to somehow capture that eternal love through words and pictures. Dorin's art is nice, and Melly's words are typically brilliant, while the choices of couples are inspired to say the least. Virginia Woolf and Victoria Sackwille - West remains a brilliant section, but my personal favourite is the part dedicated to Oscar Wilde and Lord Alfred Douglas, certainly a forbidden love in its era. In all, it's a nice but all too wistfully short book that could have done with being at least twice its length. Available for ridiculously cheap prices these days, why not pick up a second hand copy and enjoy this true oddity?

Though they do not really set the world alight, and mostly deliver the kind of goods his audience had come to expect at that point, there is the sense that sadly all of Melly's 1980s output on record is largely underrated and uncelebrated, accept for by those in the know, the Melly converts if you like. It might not have been all that hip for a teenager to be grooving to Melly in this period of new wave and new romantics, but old fans must have been comforted by the fact that Good Time George, now in his mid fifties, was still going strong and releasing decent LPs.

Like Sherry Wine saw release in 1981, another solid set consisting of standards given fresh vibrancy by their fine Chilton arrangements. With a sturdy band to back him up (Chilton of course, alongside drummer Chuck Smith, bassist Barry Dillon and pianist Bruce Boardman) Melly does what he does best and rips through some fine renditions of songs like Jerry the Junker, Way Down Yonder in New Orleans and perhaps my favourite on the album, I Wanna Hot Dog For My Roll, the latter too naughty for Melly to resist. If it's serious musical thrills you're after, then Melly's wonderful Empty Bed Blues is definitely the highlight, a song he lends a certain poignancy and irony given his busy love life. It's a fitting closer, bookended beautifully with the LP's opening cut, Wait Till You See My Baby Do the Charleston.

Though not one of his best albums, it's still worth having (all his records are), but there is no CD of this and probably never will be. (Admittedly some tracks are included on the double CD set The Pye

Jazz Anthology.) The cover itself, featuring a dapper and neatly dressed George holding up a wee glass of sherry, is one of his best.

In 1982, the constantly touring Melly, who was now also juggling TV and radio work at the same time, returned to the studio with Chilton and the Feetwarmers again for another studio record. Makin' Whoopee emerged at the back end of the year, with a sleeve by Dennis Bailey and production from the ever reliable Terry Brown.

While previous albums had gone along similar lines, this album is a little different, in that, as Melly notes on the back of the sleeve, the song choices are different to what fans might have expected previously. George writes that there was a wealth of twenties and thirties material he had neglected earlier in his career because it didn't quite fit in with what he'd previously focused on, the jazz standards familiar to most fans of the genre. The Makin' Whoopee songs had been "ignored simply because none of the great bands had got round to recording it. This album therefore reflects not only a slice of our current repertoire, but equally that extended range of mood and material which we believe has helped widen our audience."

Even though they had their work cut out locating these songs, Melly and Chilton certainly picked them well. The opener is the energetic Goody Goody, its giddiness tailor made for Melly's style, while the second track, Sporting Life, has Melly and company on swing blues form. He rips it up good and proper, his effort and sense of drive most admirable. His voice is especially strong throughout the LP, especially so on the album's title track, made famous by Eddie Cantor, but as Melly notes on the sleeve, it's "an open invitation for individual interpretation." And Melly makes good use of the opportunity to make it his own.

The twenties party atmosphere continues with the rowdy Shake Your Can, a genuine lost obscurity which they found in a list of unrecorded numbers by Andy Razaf. One of my favourite tracks is the side one closer Everybody Loves My Baby, which has some genuine excitement to it. The band are exceptional on this one, and Bruce Boardman in particular needs singling out for his glorious piano work, which helps make the music itself so authentic sounding. On side two highlights include the lovely Watch the Birdie and the bouncy and neatly done Baby Doll, which boasts a sturdy vocal effort and some excellent solos from Chilton. The sound is spare, just the piano, bass, drums and trumpet beneath Melly's vocal, and in this case the simplicity works wonders.

I Wish I Could Shimmy Like My Sister Kate is a nice jaunty one, In Melly's words, the track illustrated "another aspect we consider important and much neglected - the revival of the verse. Because of the limits imposed on them by the three and a half minute recording many bands ignored them. They are however often both charming and help, we feel, to add variety and spice to the well known numbers." Indeed, these lyrics are sublime, and Melly carries every word with clarity and faithful loyalty.

Yellow Dog Blues is one of my favourites from the LP, with its loose swing, wild trumpet and raucous drums. Melly is the song's star though, giving it some serious welly and elevating it from a simple blues jazzer to a mini Melly classic.

The new Chilton original, Bye Bye Boogie, sends the band off in style, showing that not only could John arrange the old forgotten classics and dust them off well, he could pen new material that fit in with them seamlessly. For me, it's possibly the best moment of the record. There's a great groove going on here, while the piano is especially good. Melly provides an understated vocal in keeping with the arrangement, and his words are echoed, beautifully I might add, by some colourful Chilton trumpet work.

Melly says on the back of the album that he believes it's their best record yet, and one can definitely see why he thought so. There's a tightness and unity to the sound, the song choices and the performances that makes it one of the most polished of his studio records. It's breezy, original and a breath of fresh air, with inspired material choices and top notch, show stopping performances. What more could you want?

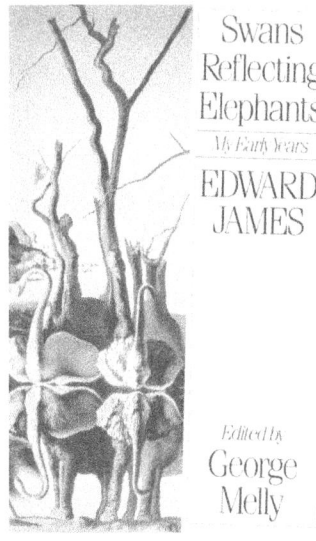

Swans Reflecting Elephants
The Early Years
EDWARD JAMES

Edited by
George Melly

While juggling touring, criticism work and recording LPs, Melly took on a rather challenging project in 1982. Edited but basically ghosted by George Melly, Swans Reflecting Elephants is among the very best work you could find in print with Melly's name attached. Basically the memoirs of the very rich and equally eccentric art collector and general encourager Edwards James, this is the kind of tale of the kind of man we will never see the like of again. James inherited the vast West Dean estate, which he turned part of into a college and also intended to preserve a Surrealistic garden there too. Eventually, as told in a fabulous 1978 documentary on him, narrated of course by George Melly, he settled in Mexico and funded the building of a surreal sculpture park which remains a popular tourist attraction to this day.

Melly states in his introduction that James was a prickly character to work with. When he realised he had accidentally taped over one of their recorded conversations, James was furious that they had to start all over again. While the resulting book is not full of Melly gems as his other titles are, James' story is definitely fascinating, though one wishes the tale itself extended beyond the eccentric's early years.

With what is probably his best album cover of the 1980s, though not the best album in my view, Melly returned with another new set of songs in 1984. The Many Moods of Melly was another solid set of reliable jazzers played and sung with a winning combination of professional efficiency and wild exuberance. The title pretty much says what it is, but then again that could be a fitting name for almost all his records. Released on PRT, this is one of the least neglected of his studio albums. Thankfully, this one is also available on CD, as are the rest of his studio albums from here on in.

It begins with the catchy Melly single Masculine Women, Feminine Men, a tidy swinger about the swappable complexities of modern sexuality. "It's hard to tell 'em apart today" he says with genuine glee. If one person could sing such a song validly, then it was certainly George Melly, well versed in the world of blurred sexuality.

Indeed, Melly shifts the mood towards a sadder, more reflective tone on It's the Bluest Kind of Blues, with George delivering a tender performance. He's pissed up and proud on Drunk Again, a real audible treat with its seamless jazz arrangement and silky vocal delivery, possibly my personal favourite on the album. It has firm competition though in the form of Kitchen Man, another decent rendition of a song he revisited many times on record and in concert.

Melly is gently on fire on St. Louis Blues, where he sings with a relaxed ease over a restless jazz backbeat. In a completely random juxtaposition of styles (hey, the album is called The Many Moods of Melly after all) Melly delivers a fabulous rendition of As Time Goes By, for my money one of the best versions, thanks in part to a simply beautiful musical backing. Still, Melly's voice is fabulous here, restrained and in control of every single note; a performance in the truest sense.

Give Her A Little Drop More had appeared on It's George ten years earlier, but Melly thought it worth doing to revisit this minor gem, giving in a touch of Skellern-esque grace in this stylish, classy rendition. "She can never be platonic," he says, "when she's had a vodka tonic," in just one of the song's wittiest lines. Melly looks even further into the past for the next track, a new version of Send Me to the 'Lectric Chair, a faithful update that more than matches up to the banned original.

Melly then returned to the land of the memoir, heading even further back into his memory bank, with 1984's childhood recollections, Scouse Mouse, featuring more essential memories from Mellydom, these ones concerning his upper middle class childhood in Liverpool. In typical Melly fashion, he penned his trilogy in reverse, staring with his 50s jazz days first and ending up in the 20s and 30s last, in 1984 in fact when he first wrote this all down. Whenever I think of this book, various images and scenarios leap out at me and lodge themselves in the weirdest corners of my mind, choosing to stay there for as long as they like. Just think of the pigs

117

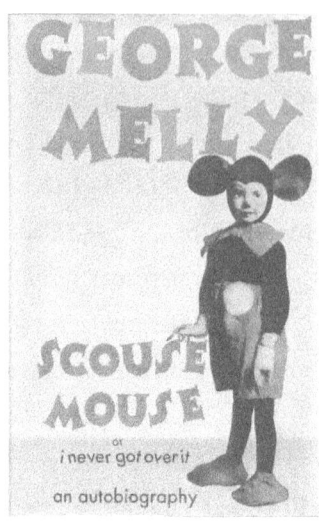

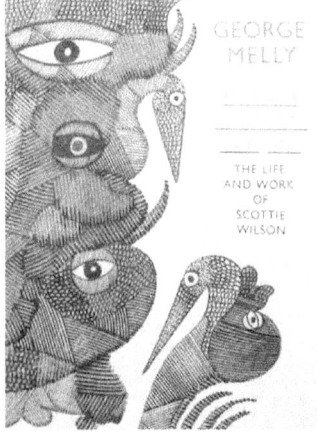

with their beady eyes staring at him from their "odoriferous pens" (brilliant writing); his mother and her gay friends; early fishing memories, like the one legged man selling worms in Holyhead. Melly describes those glory days with enthusiasm and love, even though as he says himself they often seem like random bits of film in his mind, fractured, disjointed and in no particular order. Scouse Mouse is definitely the cleanest of the memoir series, and quite often the personal favourite of many a Melly devotee.

Rather than just penning books on well known, household name artists, Melly was attracted to singing the praises of more obscure, lesser known heroes. In 1986 he wrote It's All Writ Out For You, the story of Scottie Wilson. Though it might be the name of George Melly that brings a lot of people towards this book (after all, his name on the cover ensures it's bound to be a good read, and if it's art, you know the art in question will be worthwhile), the work of Scottie Wilson, that great enigmatic outsider artist, is well worthy of your time. Yes, Melly's name is clearer and bigger on the cover than Wilson's, but that was clearly a way to attract potential admirers. Again, Melly is shedding light not on over familiar names for the sake of satisfying waves of popularity and current interest, but obscure figures on the fringes who it might be in your best interest to learn about. Personally, Wilson's work appeals to me, and it's Melly's text which props up this mysterious art and enhances its strange mythical quality.

This book features good info on Wilson, from his Scottish working class roots onwards, and is wonderfully illustrated too. I really like Wilson's work and also admire the man himself. For one, I appreciate the fact he sold his work on the street for small amounts to regular people, mistrusting the galleries and their inflated prices. He said of the working class admirers: "*They're* the intellect, you know." It's nice to know that Melly himself met Wilson and the idea of them together in one room, two very different men from different worlds, cannot fail to bring a smile to my face.

Alongside the books, touring, TV work and journalism, the albums continued to emerge. Good camp fun with Melly and Chilton, 1988's Running Wild is one of Melly's most overlooked sets. From the moment it begins it just works. Opener Sweet Georgia Brown skips along sweetly, with a fluttery arrangement and perky vocal effort, leading into the sublime and calm Hometown, one of my personal favourite Melly songs from the 80s. There's a decent go at Boogie Woogie Man again, though it's not up there with the 74 version, whereas one cannot fault the relentless grinding groove of My Momma Rocks Me, with Melly on naughty top form. But it's probably the title track that pleases the most, finishing off the album in jaunty, fun loving style, summing up the glory of Melly in his prime in four perfect minutes.

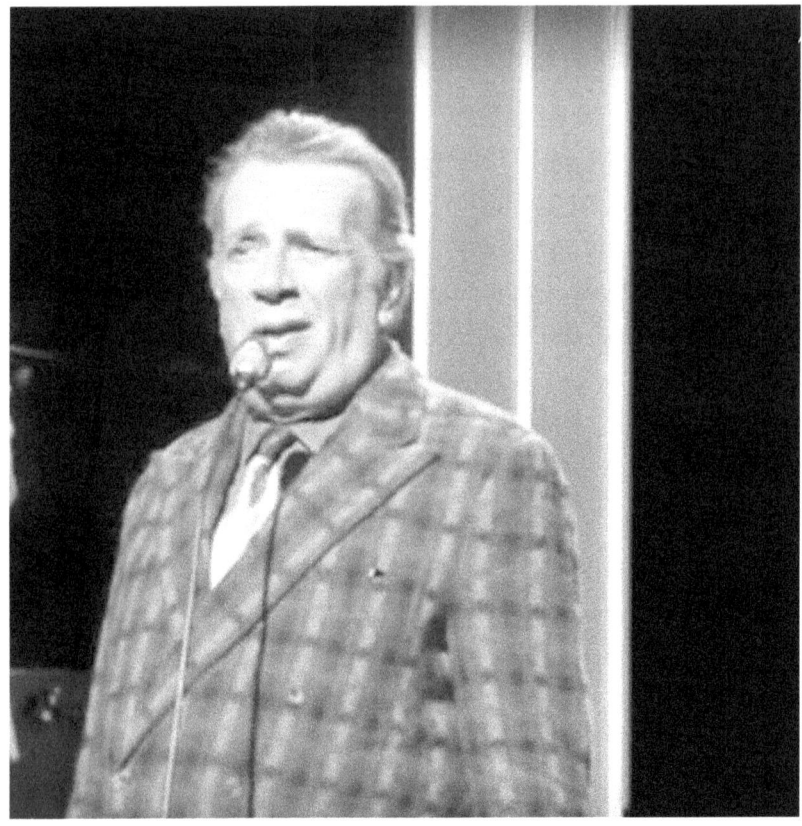

Running Wild may often get overlooked, but it's actually a sturdy set of tracks, wonderfully produced by the ever trusty Terry Brown. It maybe doesn't match up to his next LP, Anything Goes, which was one of the few Melly classics of the 70s and 80s to get both a vinyl and CD release, along with his two previous albums, The Many Moods... and Running Wild. As it happens, Anything Goes is a very solid set, which let's face it, all Melly albums are, whether recorded live or put down in the studio. On that note, it might be hard in retrospect to guide a newcomer to Melly's music because it's all so strong. As it happens, anything from the 1980s wouldn't be a bad place to begin, Anything Goes included.

The album begins with pure class with a nice easy rendition of Route 66, another song so familiar that it seems surprising that Melly can get you interested in hearing it again. But he does, and thanks to Chilton's fine arrangement, it's very easy on the ears. In fact, it's so nice I would say it's one of the best versions of the song I've heard. On the back of the record he says it's the musical equivalent of Hopper's Easy Rider or Kerouac's On the Road, though Melly's take on it is less wild and more controlled than the afore mentioned points of reference. It suits George's voice well, and though only in restrained studio form, his vocals are solid. I understand his albums do not capture the sheer magic of his live performances, but now he is gone and so little footage exists, the records and CDs are going to remain the Melly gold for years to come, and I'll continue to wax lyrical of their importance.

September Song, another standard which Melly loved to approach (he would tackle this stonker on his last album as well), is here in fine form, with the great man's vocals in their prime. The music is gorgeous, while Melly's mellow performance soars wonderfully. Everything here is pretty glorious to be honest, including the jaunty Maybe Not At All (with Melly's female impression bringing a smile to the face) and an upbeat It Had to Be You, which is genuinely effective in its swing form. Even Anything Goes, given the sleazy Melly treatment, works excellently.

The album exists in two CD versions, one just featuring the normal album and the other featuring some cuts form his next album, Puttin' on the Ritz. Opt for either, for they're both brilliant.

Though it may be predictable to say so, Puttin' on the Ritz, released in 1990, is another set you could call pure gold. Even from its cover, with a suited up Melly prancing along with a cane, you can see the album is going to be a lot of fun. With a fine band consisting of John Chilton, Ron Rubin on piano, Eddie Taylor on drums and Ken Baldock on bass, the musicianship is as tight as a Scotsman, while Melly is in fine voice throughout, though lacking a little bit of his earlier control, much envied by many singers, in certain parts.

The album begins in style with Oh Chubby Stay the Way You Are, written by Chilton, on which Melly confesses to being "a chubby chasing chancer" who likes his women round, and can't resist them if they weigh 200 pounds. One of his funniest songs, it's pure joy from beginning to end, and a great example of what a clever lyricist Chilton really was.

More serious, sombre and effective though is Melly's take on The House of the Rising Sun, which he gives the right amount of drama and dynamism, while it's Chilton's arrangement which allows Melly to ham it up good and proper. (Just listen to the gorgeous piano on this one.) Dare I say it, Melly's voice delivers the sentiments of the song, the plight of the gambling addict, better than any other I have heard, Eric Burdon included. Melly could blues it up with the best of 'em.

The album is crammed full of solid material, like Nobody Knows You (When You're Down and Out) which is pure grace and class, while another unexpected Chilton original, The Food of Love, is almost Peter Skellern-esque in its arrangement. Melly relishes the chance to play up and is having a ball over the rag time rhythm, but always pulling back and restraining enough to ensure he does not encroach over the music.

The Melly take on Puttin' on the Ritz is typically showy, the music backing him up with little fuss and allowing him to camp it up like there's no tomorrow. Hard Hearted Hannah is also a stand out, with its swinging rhythm and chilled out vocal effort. The closing track is I Don't Want to Set the World On Fire, hardly the finest moment of his recording career, but a nice finisher all the same. While Puttin' on the Ritz is no Nuts or Makin' Whoopee, it's still impossible to resist its sizeable charms... oeer obviously!

George was still writing art criticism for publications, and in 1991 he released a new book, one which should be counted with the Melly 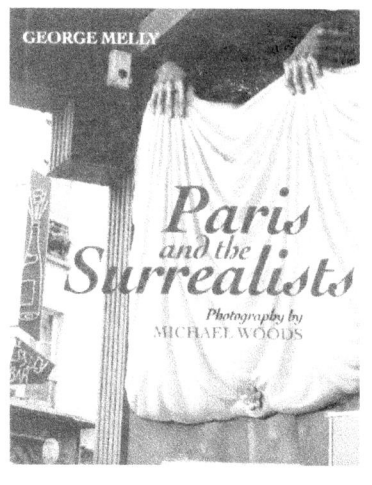 essentials. Perhaps the most beautiful to look at and stylish book in the Melly library is Paris and the Surrealists, a loving tribute to his beloved art form. Telling the history and relevance of Surrealism, the book focuses on its impact and power in Paris, and its lasting effects on the city where it was born. Andre Breton, Melly's idol and the official overlord of Surrealism, is turned into a God in Melly's lovely text, while he generally flexes his validity at being considered England's true Surrealist. It is, essentially, a pivotal and authoritative work on Surrealism. Adding to Melly's gorgeous words are the stunning photographs of London photographer Michael Woods, a friend of Melly's who was sent out to

123

take snaps of the Surreal side of Paris, which judging by Woods' pictures, is still large part of the city's culture and buzzing vibe.

Perhaps the highlight of the whole book though is Melly's remembrance of his own meeting with Breton, a pivotal moment no doubt between two Surrealistic giants; one its inventor and strict keeper, the other its eccentric adopter and loyal devotee.

In 1997, Melly appeared with a new memoir, this one possibly the most shocking of them all. Don't Tell Sybil was his recollections of working for the Belgian Surrealist ELT Mesens, and the activities they got up to in the London Gallery and beyond. There are all kinds of wonderful stories in the book itself, and Melly leaves nothing out, or indeed nothing to the imagination either. He even includes, with pride I might add, his romps with the married couple. Sexual shenanigans aside, this is a gossipy look inside the world of the Surrealists. Melly gives us stories about Rene Magritte, Edward James and a wonderful anecdote about Mesens ordering George to keep bobbing over the road to wish a new shopkeeper "good luck" over and over again, in a Surrealistic gesture to drive him up the bend. It's a bonkers book (of course, what else would you expect from Melly?) and delivers much more than its title and cover could ever hope to. But it isn't just a kiss and tell bonkathon, it's an inside story of how Melly enjoyed his time with the Surrealists and became a "man" in the truest sense. It's a vital read in understanding the many varied sides of the George Melly prism.

To promote the book, George appeared on various chat shows, one of which Chanel 5's long dead 5's Company. Clearly scaring the shit out of the hosts in case he says anything outrageous, Melly gave them exactly what they wanted... and more. He talks about his discovery of the wonderful world of pussy, pockets a handful of chocolates from the table, promises to get some more on the way out and generally skirts over the edge of decency. Watching the old clip reminds us that we really don't get fun people like George on the telly anymore.

George was always a regular on TV (in the 80s he had his Good Time George show, and before and after he appeared on various arts and film shows), but he had some particularly memorable TV turns in the 1990s. Pure gold is the wonderful Melly episode of This is Your Life, with Michael Aspel surprising George in Edinburgh, then brining before him his wife and kids, friends, girlfriends even, and a few old jazz friends. He even closes it off with a performance of Dr Jazz.

As the 1990s drew to a close, Melly entered the new millennium, a changing time for the world and certainly for him too. There would be big shifts in the next few years, both professionally and personally, though some were more impactful than others.

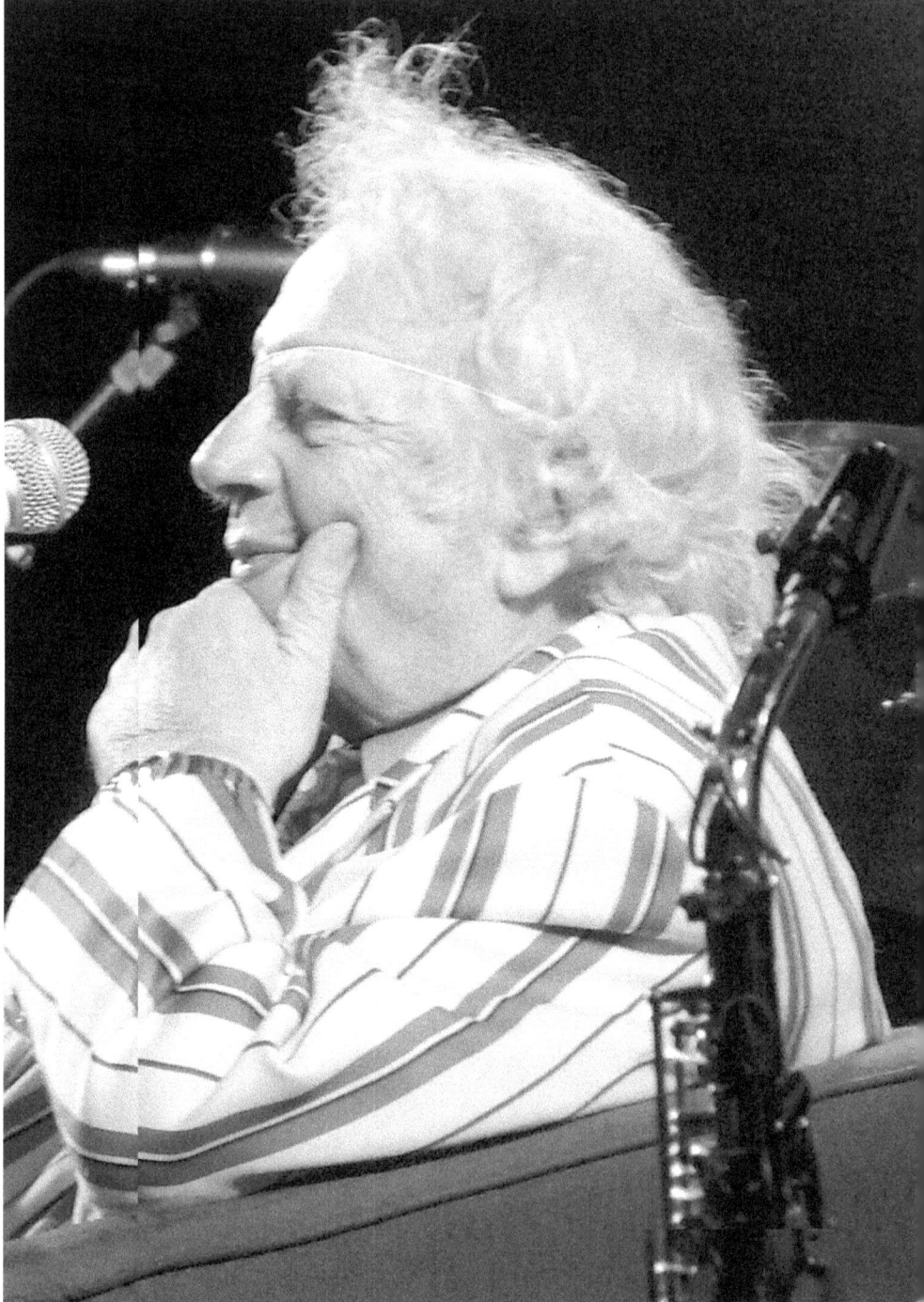

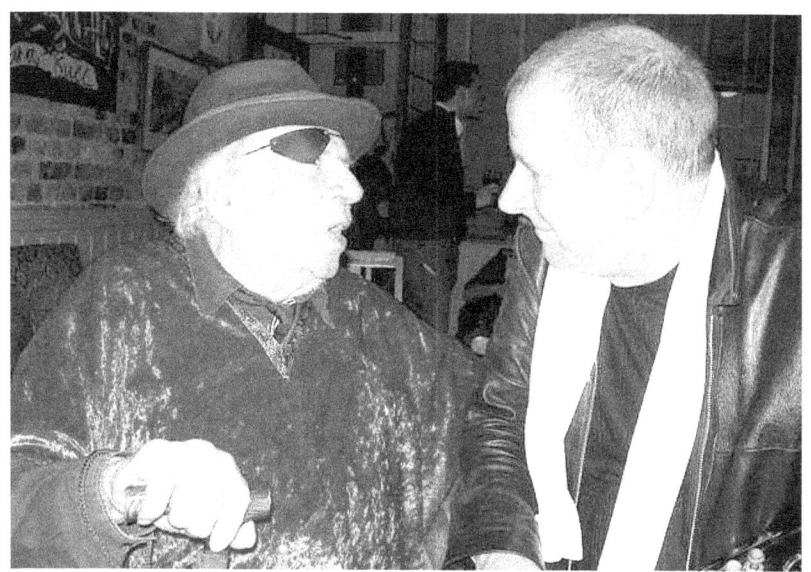

THE FINAL YEARS

"Death is no longer either a distant phenomenon or a timely accident, and the time allotted is inevitably short and growing shorter by the minute. What's left is far less than what is past, and I am on parole."

How did Melly begin the new millennium? Well, rather unexpectedly, with a fishing memoir, recounting all the joys and glories of his side "career" as a keen fisherman. Although it might garner a groan or two, but Hooked is definitely the most fitting title George could have come up with for his witty and very engaging fishing memoir. While I am not remotely interested in fishing (but would never dare to utter the cliché "I don't think I have the patience for it," which so frustrated Melly) I was fascinated by his sheer passion and love for the sport, hobby or whatever one might want to call it. While it didn't make me want to take up fishing, it did make me want to go fishing with George Melly, maybe just to sit and listen to him while he did the casting and reeling in. Anyone as disinterested in fishing in me might be put off by the book, but fear not, it's as funny and unputdownable as his earlier books. It's occasionally hilarious, constantly addictive and at one point typically Mellyian. And it is this most Melly-esque moment which has stuck with me the most for some reason - the early confession that he once wanked into a dock leaf after a big catch. If that isn't a typical George Melly anecdote, I don't know what is!

Despite still being larger than life and as recognisable as any person can possibly be, in his later years George Melly did slow down a little, though not by personal choice. He enjoyed fishing, but then he always had, but as an older gentleman it took precedence over other, wilder activities. "Over jazz," he said in 2000, "fishing just has the edge." He was serious about his fishing, that's for sure. At one point Melly even sold some of his beloved artworks to pay for a stretch of his favourite fishing spot, the River Usk, just in case they sold it off and he was ever unable to fish there. With his country retreat in Brecon, Wales, George found time to unwind and escape the dizzying world of fame and jazz.

However, as he entered his seventies, ill health began to limit his life style and take hold of him, though he still put men half his age to shame with his schedule and sheer passion. "I don't do anything different except what nature has forbidden me," Melly said in 2005. "I drink a bit less because I don't want to bounce off the walls and have to be pushed upstairs. I had to give up smoking a few years ago because they were a bit dodgy about my lungs. I, of course, go through all the things that old people do anyway - memory, lack of a sense of time passing. I say to a young person 'Remember that film?' and my wife says 'Of course they don't... that was 25 years ago'."

At the age of 65 in the early 90s, Melly wrote a fabulous article about the arrival of old age. "When I was asked to write this piece," he wrote, "I proposed it should describe the diminution of my once over-active libido, but something about that worried me. It came to me just in time, almost pen in hand: in a recent interview for a newspaper, and on the radio, I had banged on about the same subject in depth. Memory and repetition are two traitors, two mutineers. The first, rat-like, leaves the sinking ship, the second takes over the wheel. The time has come perhaps to admit that my awareness of my end, my old masterish contemplation of a skull, albeit wearing a false moustache or bowler hat, was activated by a crisis. Eight months ago, waiting for the band to show up in a dressing room of the Colchester Theatre, I was knocked to the ground by a bleeding ulcer, my legs kicking out in all directions. As I lay there, I thought to myself: 'This is it then.' It was, after all, an ulcer which had killed my father and my grandfather, both in their sixties. Why shouldn't I go the same way? Only I didn't. I was singing again 10 days later. They've got ulcers (if caught in time) licked now. I'm feeling much better than I did before"

Time was passing though and things were about to change. When John Chilton put his trumpet in his case for good and vowed to retire and take it easy, Melly had to search for a new right hand man. One day he found one in Digby Fairweather. The roots of the link between Melly and his fellow jazz man went back to the mid sixties, when Digby was working as a junior assistant in a library in Southend On

Sea. By his own admission, Melly's fabulous jazz memoir Owning Up became a kind of guide book for him in his early jazz days, a "behavioural vade-mecum, a raver's primer." Would he have thought that nearly forty years later, at the start of the new millennium, he would be touring and recording with Melly, the legendary Surrealist Jazzer himself? Clearly not, for no one could see that coming.

While Digby got on with his adventures with George, both men were taking notes for their own respective books. Melly's was entitled Slowing Down, a classy, beautifully written and rather moving memoir of his elder years, including various adventures with Digby and his Half Dozen group. Digby's own book, On the Road With George Melly, emerged very soon after his death (maybe a little too soon some say) but seemed like a fitting tribute to this fine man who had touched all our lives, Digby's included of course.

Fairweather goes into detail in his book about his fondness for Melly and states that though they had a lot in common - their shared love of writing and Noel Coward, their middle class backgrounds, their rebellious streaks - he also admits that he couldn't help but feel he would have enjoyed working with Melly when he was younger, and would have taken part in even richer chats with the aging icon, before the deafness took hold and dominated communication. Still, he was a "friend and fellow thinker" to the end. Fairweather also found they had a deeper mental link, an instinctive intuition when it came to music and especially adlibs. They were both, Digby admits, often pissed as farts on stage together, which only added to the chaotic magic of latter day Melly.

For Digby, getting to work with Melly was both an honour and a convenient turn of luck. He'd received a phone call from the promoter Jack Higgins, who informed him that John Chilton and the Feetwarmers were retiring and asked if he would he be willing to fill the gap and become the musical sideman for George. This gig would also include his Half Dozen band, who had been going for eight years at that point and were struggling to keep afloat on the live circuit. Melly's proposal ensured him a career and a living, and seeing as he was already an admirer, how was he going to seriously refuse the invite? Digby called Chilton to get his blessing, who then sent Digby a typed out letter listing all of Melly's repertoire.

It may have been a huge step up for Digby and his group, but it must have been troubling and daunting for Melly, who had spent thirty years with Chilton and the boys, and had learned all their musical quirks, strengths and particulars. But here he was, in his mid seventies, after three decades of cosy musical togetherness with a musical soul mate, having to say goodbye to his right hand man and head out to uncharted seas in search of a new band of pirates to aid him in his next chapter. In Fairweather though, Melly knew he had found a good man for the job.

When Digby first spoke to George on the phone he invited him for dinner. Carrying a bottle of booze, Digby visited him at home, where a blue clad Melly answered the door and let him in. Judging by his account, it seems he was over awed ever so slightly by the Melly magic, the surreal artwork on the walls, and the general vibe of his haunt. Pretty soon though, the two chaps became familiar, and began to take up the engagements that the tiring Chilton could no longer find the energy to fulfil. They gigged furiously, recorded albums and spent hours talking to fans after shows, signing books, CDs and records.

The first album Melly made with Digby and his Half Dozen band came in 2003 with the excellent Singing and Swinging the Blues. The album begins with the energetic The Joint is Jumpin', which has Melly in vital form, even though the power is beginning to dim ever so slightly. Still, the bounce of the music gives it a force which compliments the tones of the hard living veteran.

Ol' Rockin' Chair is an old classic here transformed into a self referential song of poignancy, especially when considering the "Mr Melly" introduction and his increased years. His voice is still pure, but slightly weathered, yet he is far from bowing out just yet. The increased pace of the rhythm injects a certain reserved joy into this rather moving, strangely emotional arrangement.

There are loads of great songs here, sung with typical gusto and depth by Melly. I Can't Get Started With You is so raw and exposed it almost hurts, while Melly trademarks like the old Dr Jazz are given a new lease of life. The band is exceptional, it has to be said, and Digby's guys definitely deserve a lot of the credit for this album's success. Still, Melly is the voice and essentially the focal point of the frolicking fun.

Other tracks are even improved upon, like the more groovy and crunchy version of Frankie and Johnny, which sounds fabulous with its deep brass, loose drums, spots of guitar work and smooth organ sounds, not to mention the full Melly vocal. Trouble in Mind is Melly in full on blues mode, while moments like Trombone Cholly are pure joy personified. The rendition of T'ain't Nobody's Bizness If I Do is pure gold, the arrangement effortlessly easy on the ears, propping up a charismatic vocal performance from Our Man George at his best. Possibly the finest and most arresting song here is the closer,

132

George's take on September Song, which is transformed into a pained reflective moment in the shade, a few minutes of calm in an otherwise turbulent and mad storm. Anyone afraid that Digby might not be able to replace John Chilton as arranger and do Melly's voice justice need not worry; this is a superb album, arranged and put together with sheer professionalism and heart felt passion. A joy from start to finish, pure and simple.

Ultimate Melly is perhaps the finest of the three Digby and George team ups, on pure musical terms, in that it has more genuine glee to

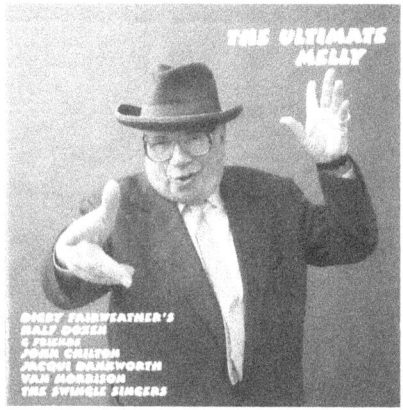

it. Granted all three are great, but there is something so "right" about this collection that there is no way it shouldn't be listed up there among Melly's finest collections.

It begins, remarkably enough, with a duet with Van Morrison himself. Van the Man sounds tremendous as usual on Midnight Cannonball, but when put aside the roaring power of George Melly, even he sounds like something of a whimperer. Van is one of the greatest singers of modern music, but it's a testament to Melly's sheer power and strength that he should, though not consciously, blow Van right out of the mix.

While some of the sung intros are a bit corny, they also add a nice bit of humour. But it's in Melly's unmistakable tones where the real magic dwells. Kitchen Man, another old Melly wonder, is given new life here, only a year before the great man's death, while Everybody

Loves My Baby is a little slice of magic, closer to heavy rock in parts than jazz with its neat guitar and punchy arrangement.

There is lighter fluff as well, like Melly's duet with Jacqui Dankworth, Let's Call the Whole Thing Off, which is pretty charming in itself and you'd have to be a real misery guts not to get some pleasure from. Smoother moments stick out too, like God Bless the Child, which is strangely magical, with its fluttering back drop, sweet piano, sweeping strings and up close and personal vocal. Gone Fishin' is pure eccentric joy, with Melly referencing his own love of fishing above a measured musical back drop, and the fact he's slowing down. "Chilled out," George says. Slightly cheesy yes, but also impossible not to love. The more bouncy stuff is excellent too, like the rock n' roll frantic shuffle of Roll 'Em Pete which brings to mind that old classic The Boogie Woogie Man. Though his voice is dying out on As Time Goes By, the emotion and passion is still there, as it is on the whole of the record. The finale is the lighter The Trudge, which closes the album off in style.

The Sunday Times enjoyed the record and found it a lot of fun. "Quite why the grand old trouper is the bête noire of so many jazzers is one of life's mysteries. He has done plenty to push the music into the mainstream, and has never taken himself as seriously as some of the critics take themselves. Just as his latest volume of memoirs, Slowing Down, strolls genially through the trials of old age, his studio bash with a new accomplice, Digby Fairweather, offers the equivalent of a late-night shot of whisky. Melly is no longer a hellraiser, but his sense of mischief remains intact."

But that wasn't it for Digby and George's adventures on CD. Farewell Blues, Melly's official send off, came out in 2007, the year of his death. There was another title released a year after his death, First and Last, but it was a compilation put out in a limited edition of 1000 in aid of a dementia charity. Farewell Blues, in many ways, is one of the most poignant and moving albums of George's whole career. It's often a sad listen, but ultimately comes across as a worthwhile, somewhat poetic goodbye to an icon.

There's some undoubtedly strong material here. Salty Dog is charm personified, with a characterful Melly vocal, while this new version of Empty Bed Blues is a total killer. Some of the nicest parts on the CD are the interludes where Melly reminisces. Whereas his singing voice might have been croaky in parts at this stage (the man was dying after all) these spoken word parts are flawless, and Melly holds every bit of your concentration with his fond recollections. The first one is looking back to his schooldays, his early love of Bessie Smith and when he was getting into jazz big time. The story about his old Landlord, as featured in his book Owning Up, is fabulous, with Melly reading out the upset Landlord's rather long and intricate letter about what a terrible lodger he really is. Judging by his fair criticisms of Melly's life style at the time, you have to say old Bill Meadmore had a point. George's memories of joining Mick Mulligan are wonderful too, as are his remembrances of going pro with John Chilton and the Feetwarmers. With these lovely sections placed between tracks, the album takes an almost funereal atmosphere, and in many ways it feels like a wake where the deceased has managed to somehow read out his own life story for the gathered mourners. A most surreal experience it is.

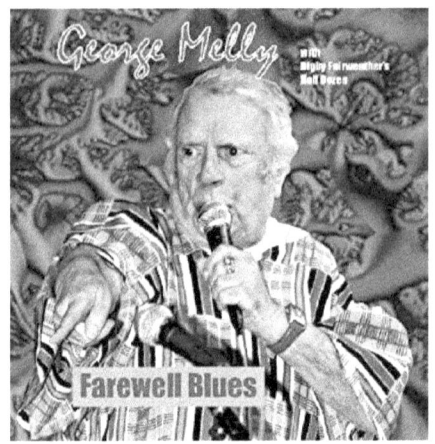

Elsewhere the songs are so damn good that the album deserves its "farewell" status, with staggering versions of Send Me to the 'Lectric Cahir, an early Melly classic from the old days, and a sharp and concise Young Woman's Blues. Throughout the album George sings his heart out with admirable passion, and even though he is clearly beginning to slide down hill, not for one moment does the album become a pitiful affair. In fact, his voice often sounds stronger than it had on The Ultimate Melly, and perhaps even than on his and Digby's first outing. One only has to listen to the sheer joys of this new version of I Need A Little Sugar In My Bowl to learn that Melly may have been slipping away from this world, but his determination to keep on singing had remained untouched. A stonking performance.

Brother's Blues is a fabulous end, with Melly reflecting on his Mulligan days, sending us off in style, backed up by a rather haunting echo laden, almost ghostly trumpet which highlights the length of George's journey in jazz, still singing and jiving away right to the end. As the song moves into its warm brass section, one cannot help but be genuinely moved by the sentiments, the fact that Melly is on his way to the pearly gates. Just wait though, fast forward a minute or so and you get a vintage recording of Rock Island Line sung with typical gusto by a youthful and spirited George Melly in his twenties. It ends, fittingly enough, where it all started.

That's not quite it for George's discography though. His studio and live albums aside, there are also a host of Melly compilations out there too, some old, some more recent, others released after his death. The first proper Melly "hits" collection so to speak came in 1973, when Decca released a collection of his fifties songs under the name The World of George Melly. The cover, featuring Melly in a vest looking a little inebriated, is certainly eye catching, and the material on the set is worthy of such a grand sleeve. Old classics like Heebie Jeebies, Abdul Abulbur Amir and Send Me to the 'Lectric Chair are needed on any serious Melly collector's shelf, and though they are available in other forms and formats, it's nice to have them included on a "World Of..." set. (These albums are wonderful to collect, featuring every one from Pete and Dud to Alan Price.)

There are plenty of good compilations out there on CD too. The Ravers set, credited to Mick Mulligan and His Jazz Band also features some mid 50s Melly singles, while the Live release from 2002 groups together the cuts they did for Tempo, previously included on their compilation samplers. More essential though are Melly collections like The Best of George Melly, released in the early 90s, and Good Time George, a 2001 CD issue of the World Of album.

After the early 90s, most of what was coming out was a compilation in some form. While in the 1970s and 80s new Melly records had appeared almost every year or two, by the 1990s they were scarce. Puttin' on the Ritz was to be the last studio album released in his own name, and it would be a decade until he teamed up with Digby Fairweather for the final chapter. That said, there are CD issues in the 90s which are worthy of your purchase. Though officially a compilation, the 1995 Best of Live CD is another winner. Available

137

only on CD, it features a host of Melly classics, sung live with typical gusto and backed up by John Chilton and the Feetwarmers. The versions of Melly staples like Boogie Woogie Man (here sounding just fabulous), My Canary Has Circles Under His Eyes and Ain't Misbehavin', the whole thing is a joy and presents Melly at his best and the top of his game. Chilton ain't too shabby either. The CD

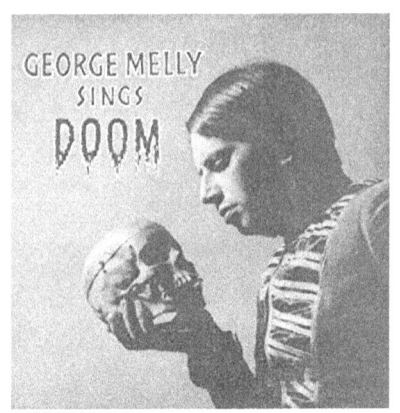

proved to be a kind of swan song for Melly and Chilton's musical adventures. It was in the late 90s and early 2000s that Chilton began to slow down and lose interest in their mad touring schedule, being replaced by Fairweather.

Even after his death, new compilations began to appear. In 2008, Sporting Life emerged, complete with blue tinted image of a mid performance Melly in full flight. The fact it was just another reissue of the World Of album was rather disappointing, but anyone let down by the fabulous Cherry Red 2014 release of George Melly Sings Doom, a compilation of his 50s Decca recordings, needs their head testing. When the album came out, some seven years after his death, people seemed to stop and take notice of Melly once again, and many reviewers elevated him to one of the great jazz singers Britain ever produced.

"When discussing George Melly, the phrase 'we won't see his like again' remains a legitimate cliché," Record Collector wrote. "But we rarely saw his like even when he was alive. Scholarly and sincere in obeisance to his trad jazz and blues forebears, Melly nevertheless played to the gallery with boggle-eyed extravagance, sticking his bum out like a mandrill. Sings Doom collates A-sides, B-sides and EP tracks Melly recorded for Decca and Tempo between 1952 and 1959, and a blowzy trad tonic it is. As with Donald McGill postcards, some of the euphemisms deployed herein are so blatant as to retain a measure of shock value: Organ Grinder, Ma Rainey's Black Bottom, You've Got The Right Key But The Wrong Hole. In each, the trombone-voiced Melly tips a wink as broad as a lighthouse beam. Delightfully, he tackles the titular "doom" selections (Cemetery Blues, Death Letter, Send Me to the 'Lectric Chair) with much the same epicurean relish."

The George Melly discography at one point must have been a tasking thing to complete, but given the widespread variety of the internet, it's pretty easy (and affordable) these days to complete your Melly collection. There are a reasonable amount of studio albums, but not too, any, and I can safely say they are all worth buying for different reasons. Not a single one is a dud, and you can't say that about many artists. The compilations may be a little harder to navigate through, but pick wisely and you will be rewarded with Melly riches.

Melly may have jazzed it to the end, but it wasn't the only one of his obsessions he kept on for as long as possible. Surrealism remained a passion, even if he felt like the last man standing at times. As an old man Melly seemed to think Surrealism as a movement was almost dead, and that there were very few Surrealists still limping about. "I can't be a Surrealist because there is no group any more. I see the Surrealists that are still alive. Not too many, alas. And I study it all the time. It was an amazing period and Breton, the leader, was a charismatic figure. He was called the Pope of Surrealism, but a friend of mine, an art critic called David Sylvester, now dead, said: 'No, Georgie. Not the Pope of Surrealism, the Saint of Surrealism'. He was very pure, and what the Surrealists did outside his watchful eye was often not at all pure by his standards."

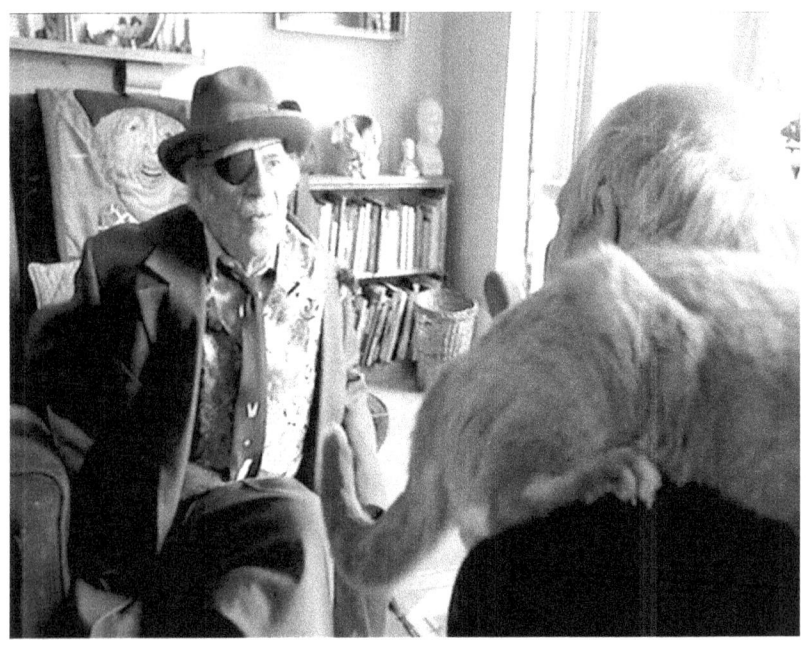

Alan Yentob, scarved by Melly's cat, sits before his Surrealist guru.

Ultimately though, Melly saw that Surrealism had been misunderstood and swallowed up by the cynicism of modern times, in aid of commerce and profit. He was, as the inventor of the modern idea of Surrealism Andrew Breton had been, a total puritan when it came to his beloved Surrealism. "I think superficial aspects of Surrealism penetrate everything, including advertisements for

Benson and Hedges. The meaning of Surrealism, its philosophical position, the attempt to fuse the subconscious and conscious, to make them one strata of thought, the search for complete freedom, is alas not very important to most people. And goodness knows one doesn't live the surrealist life oneself. Surrealism is an historical movement which is very important and I think it said a lot of things that needed saying. Of course it got itself into an almost impossible position because it tried to be effective politically and was rejected by all politicians as a hopeless sort of anarchic dream. You have read the history of Surrealism and the Communist Party. It was a tragicomedy first class. But I think Surrealism survived and I breathe the Surrealist air with gratefulness. But I am someone who sticks to the reassuring moments of revolt in my youth."

In the afore mentioned Surreal Thing documentary, Alan Yentob seems slightly saddened, or moved at least, by the sight of the frail Melly. Still in his zoot suit, purple and typically Mellyian, eye patch and all, he looks like the world's last Surrealist, flying the flag even as the ship goes down. "You may know George Melly as a jazz singer," he said, "but for me he's a mentor and guide to the subterranean kingdom of Surrealism." Indeed, for me, though Melly's music reaches places few others in the jazz field ever could, he will remain the UK's most quintessential, pure, eccentric and magical Surrealist. Surrealism is dead. Long live Surrealism. And long live George Melly...

We are all mortal and when Melly's time came, he went with it with admirable bravery, facing death straight on and refusing to cringe and wince. Melly outright refused any treatment, saying that it would make him too tired to work. Then Diana found out he had dementia, which was only going to get worse. Yet George insisted on doing more gigs, some up north, which did his confused state no good at all. Naturally, Diana became increasingly more worried about him. In the end, she got the doctor to write a note to state that gigs outside the local area were a no-no.

Then, at the age of 79, Melly wrote another memoir, this one turning out to be his last. Although it's his least intense and urgent in many ways, Slowing Down is possibly my personal favourite of all his

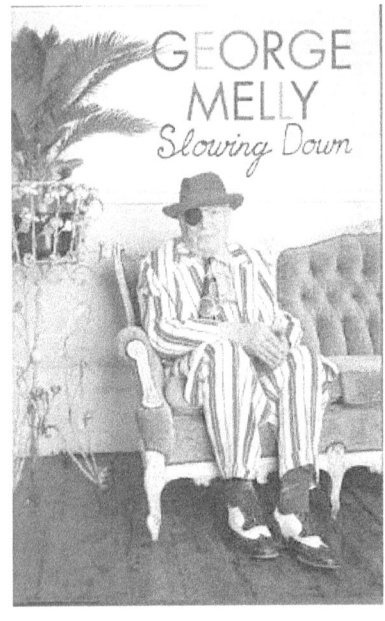

books, but not for straight forward reasons. It was written while his health was ailing, but he was still fully aware of what was going on around him, even if his memory and hearing were rapidly going more and more down hill. The resulting book, at times sad, at times moving, but always raw and honest, is also totally lacking in vanity, boastfulness or arrogance. This is a man fully aware that pretty soon he is going to be on his last legs, and he is refreshingly frank and accepting of this fact.

What is most surprising is how George makes routine check ups and hospital visits entertaining. He also waxes lyrical on modern life, though never becomes preaching or boring, and looks back at his past to the Chilton era, his adventures with the colourful Derek Taylor and his memories of Ronnie Scott. In all, it feels like you've spent a few hours with George, and he's decided to discuss random events and phases of his life. A beautiful, wonderful, enlightening book, which is both poignant and warm, as well as being a master class in autobiography. National treasure is an awful phrase, but after reading this book you'll understand why Melly deserves that title.

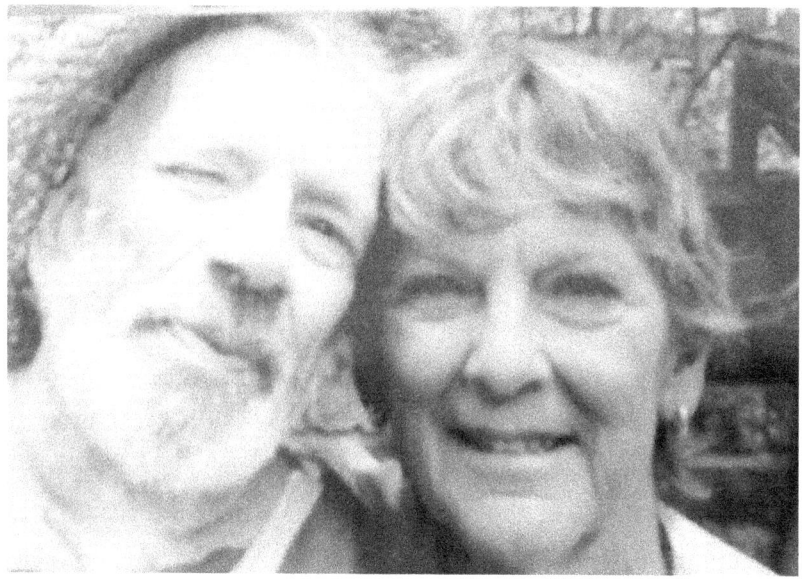

But Melly's mind began to weaken, and his behaviour grew more bizarre. He would obsess over details, like whether peas had been served with his meal or not. He would speak of three lovely women floating through his room to his en suite bathroom, and the fact he had been cast as Jesus Christ in an upcoming movie. "You're nearly 80 and Jesus died when he was 30," Diana gently told him. "Must be kind of a weird film." Still, despite this confusion, or perhaps because of it, he said that as a Surrealist he was delighted to have dementia.

His last show was at the 100 Club in aid of Diana's dementia charity work, a fitting send off for sure. They both hoped that the cancer would kill him before the dementia, and indeed it did. When George died in July of 2007 at the age of 80, his doctor told Diana, "That was the best death I've ever seen."

Melly's life was rich, colourful and very multi faceted indeed. The straight faced Surrealist one sees on the Arena documentary is a world away from the bawdy, smutty, fun loving jazz singer he was on stage, again a very different man to the wise critic he was for various newspapers and arts publications. Mutli-talented, Melly was able to apply his charisma, magnetism and good humour to any and every area he approached. It was that rare cross over appeal he had that very few possess. As a broadcaster he was hard to beat, with his Jazz Greats series and art shows beyond compare. As a performer he was up with the best, injecting a bit of va va voom into the often sombre world of jazz. His very name sums up excess, hard living and hedonism, and hearing his songs always brings a smile to my face. He's the kind of Renaissance man we don't celebrate anymore, in these times of mobile phones, social media and brain dead TV. No doubt if Melly were here he'd be puzzled by how much the world has dumbed itself down, even in the eleven years since his death, and shake his head at the cultural void our country has now entered. On the other hand, who knows how he might have felt. He may have popped up in Celebrity Big Brother, amusing fellow guests with anecdotes; or shown up on I'm A Celebrity Get Me Out Of Here, eating kangaroo testicles with glee. After all, Good Time George was unpredictable, and that's what made him unique.

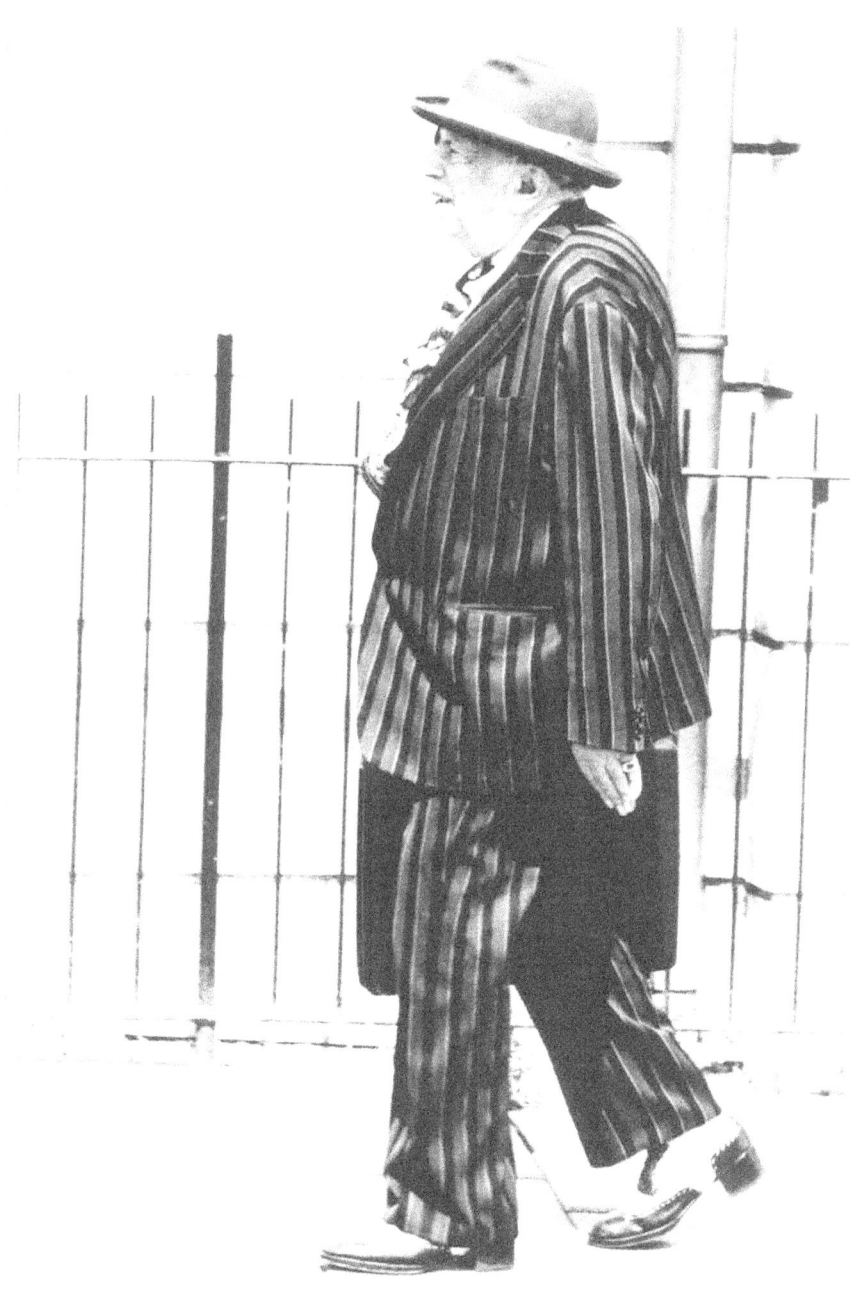

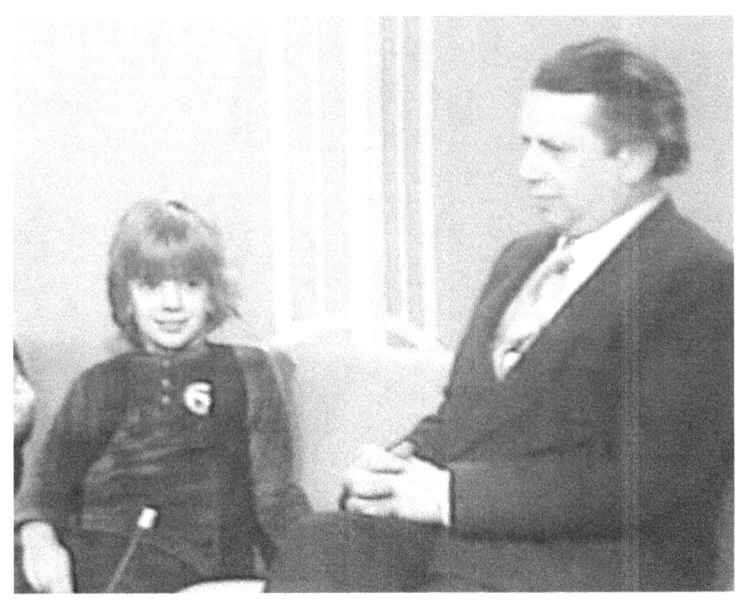

AN INTERVIEW WITH TOM MELLY

George's son Tom was born in the mid sixties, just as his mother and father settled down together and got married and George was in the midst of his full time writing phase. Given he was there in George's life until the end, it seemed rather daft not to speak to him about his dad and get his view on things. I rang him up one day and was instantly struck by his tonal similarities to his father. He is his own man though, that much is clear from only a few words, but he recalls his father with fondness and warmth.

I was interested in something you said during the BBC Last Stand documentary, about you being rather embarrassed when Rum, Bum

and Concertina came out. What was it like growing up with this man who was larger than life as a father?

Yeah. Most of the time it was rather enjoyable. As far as I remember, when the book came out was the only time I was slightly on edge, because it was just an unfortunate age to be "outed" as it were as having a gay dad, or a dad who used to be gay, I must have been about 14 I am guessing, and he was perpetually appearing on chat shows promoting the book, these evening magazine programmes. So everyone at boarding school would be going 'Oh your dad's on telly tonight,' and I'd be going, 'Oh shit, he's going to be talking about being gay during the navy.' But aside from that I didn't have any issues; and even that was just an issue of potential peer embarrassment, rather than any discomfort I had with his choice of lifestyle. So yeah it was just a tense week or so while he was doing the book promotion rounds, as it were. But as far as I can remember, when he was on the shows the subject didn't come up in conversation, presumably because it was on at 6 o'clock, and I think the interview guidelines were stricter then. The BBC might have been nervous about promoting anything to do with homosexuality, under that Section 28 bollocks (a Thatcher enforced act of banning the promotion of homosexuality). But yeah, he did occasionally embarrass me in public, but that was more to do with his default flirtation with any woman he went near, or came near him, irrespective of whether I was there or not. Particularly as I grew older and I could see what he was doing, I saw it was a constant thing. 'I will make a pass at this attractive woman, because that is what I do.' That was his default but it wasn't aggressive or unpleasant or groping, but nevertheless fairly blatant what he was doing. I kind of found that a bit much in the end. But that is really the only gripe about him really. The Rum, Bum and Concertina thing was more a moment of embarrassment.

So you still had your conventional dad moments, if conventional is a word we can really use...

Yeah, I mean, who knows... With the dad I had, everything seemed conventional to me. It didn't really occur to me. We all grew up in Gloucester Crescent, which was a kind of enclave of similar types of people. There was Jonathan Miller and Alan Bennett. It was the kind of street where one grew up expecting one's neighbours to be on telly now and then. Even in the context of where we lived it didn't seem unusual. It was only later that I realised what a peculiar environment it was, or an exceptional one.

I wanted to ask about his writing too. I looked in the ELT Mesens book and you have a dedication in there. Did you have anything to do with the research for that one?

Not the research, but I did all the typing and initial editing. You know, I'd say, 'that's awful, what are you saying here? Do you want a comma here?' So I did that. At the time I had learned to touch type, and we had a word processor, so I certainly typed out Paris and the Surrealists and the ELT Mesens one. Those are the two I remembered mostly. I was able to pick up on some of his worst habits and some of the bad ones that crept into his writing. We did the same with Scouse

Mouse, I think we all picked over the first draft for him. We encouraged him to do changes.

I love his writing. His style is so smooth and seamless, but was a lot of it down to good editing?

Yeah. But it was more that he had a streak of sentimentality, rather mawkish sentimentality that he would indulge. The one I remember in Scouse Mouse, there was this passage. It must have been after his mother died, not that he was particularly thrown by that because he wasn't thrown by anything really, but the one I remember was this passage about him seeing a squirrel and a pram in Sefton park, and saying 'I wonder where that squirrel's bones lie now,' and it was like 'Who gives a shit?'

That is a weird little detail.

Yeah. He did have a sentimental side to him. He wasn't emotional, but he was sentimental. He was not emotional in the way that he rarely engaged his emotions with other people. That wasn't what he was. He was a talker and a kind of thinker. As far as sentimentality goes, it was definitely that over emotion.

I suppose that kind of emotion ties in with his Surrealism in a way.

Yes, I think so. He had quite a clinical approach to life, which seems rather unusual for someone who was so flamboyant and eccentric. I don't think he was boring, but he didn't dig very deep into himself. It was very much about the surface of things. You got to know him very quickly. He was very agreeable and gregarious, but that was it, you didn't really get to know much more about him, no matter how many years you stuck with him. He was a sort of enigma. His emotional life was as much as an enigma to himself as it was to anyone else. I mean he managed to have his heart broken the first time when he was about fifty. And that was it, he'd escaped unscathed until then due to this weird emotional resilience.

He seems to have been very disciplined in his work ethic too, while also being a wild man.

Yeah. When he first went back on the road in the 70s he was drinking excessively while on stage, and it kind of worked to a point, because his fans loved it. You know, him falling under the piano and falling asleep and the band leader having to say 'I am afraid the captain is no longer in charge of the ship.' But he certainly cut back. He was generally rather pissed by the end of the evening and the gig. He was probably an alcoholic, although he'd never call himself that. But he probably was.

I was wondering if he got you interested in Surrealism at all?

Yes to a degree. I love surreal art, and I love any good art. But I wasn't as into it as he was. I remember when he filmed the BBC Arena special on Surrealism, as a kind of treat I was allowed to go with him for the filming, with the young Alan Yentob. I remember I got to meet The Stranglers as well, which was great. They were supposed to be playing the gang that he meets down the alley which he scares off by reciting Kurt Schwitter, but they didn't want to be seen doing anything violent, so they just appeared as themselves. I always remember my dad coming up with the idea of filming this pumping station where you could see the trees reflected on the glass so it looked like they were inside the building, and then Yentob claimed it as his own idea. My dad always went on about that, 'That Yentob claiming my ideas as his own.' So that was good, watching all that being filmed.

What about near the end? Did you find his death difficult?

No not really. He was ill, it was his time, and he died and that was it. I felt OK about it. I had all good memories of him. I think he and my mum had a kind of reconciliation of sorts at the end. Not that they had fallen out, they had always had an understanding, but she was able to push everything aside at the end and care for him. And his funeral was such a fun, jovial affair; that stopped it all from being too sad for me.

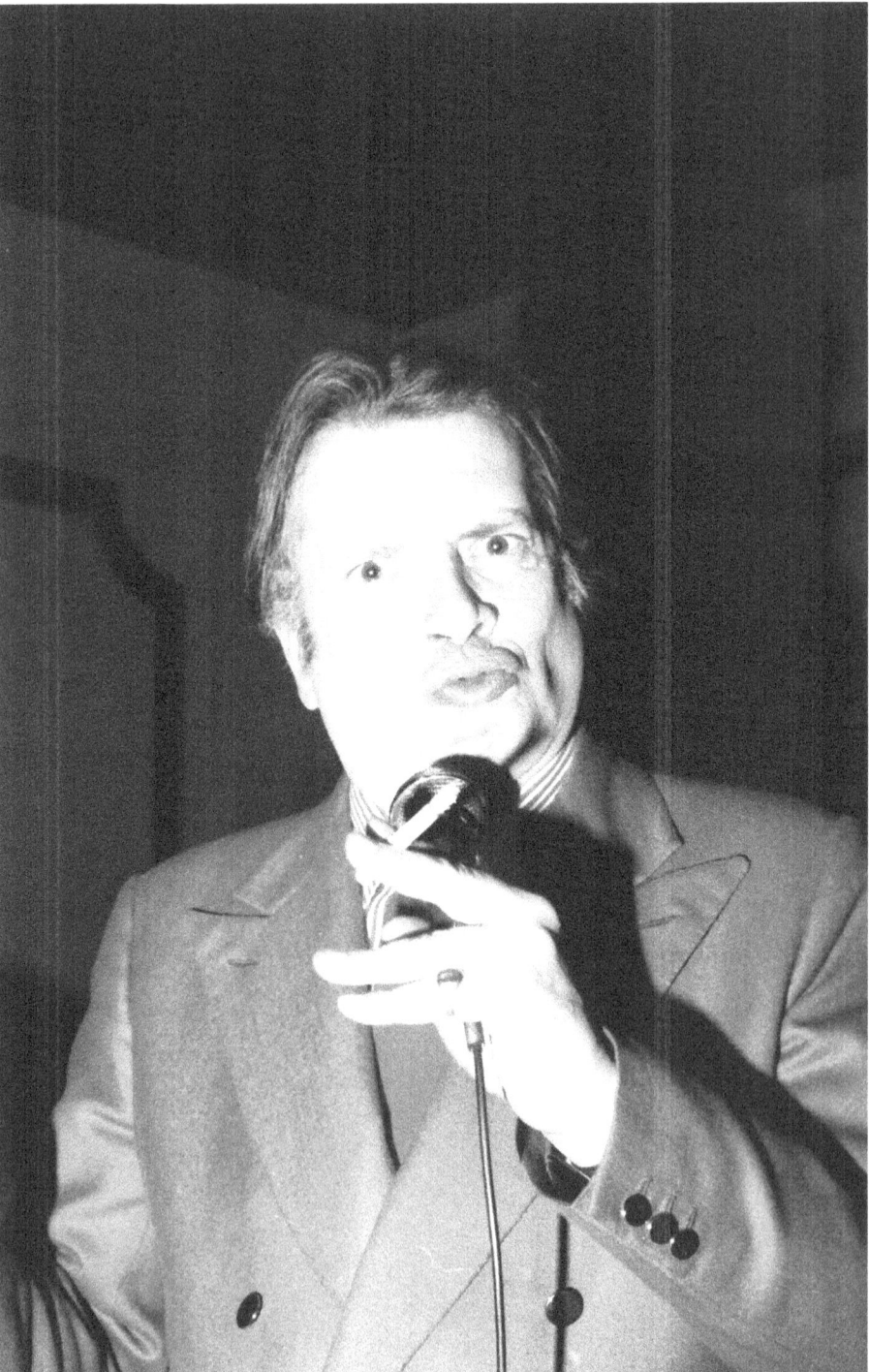

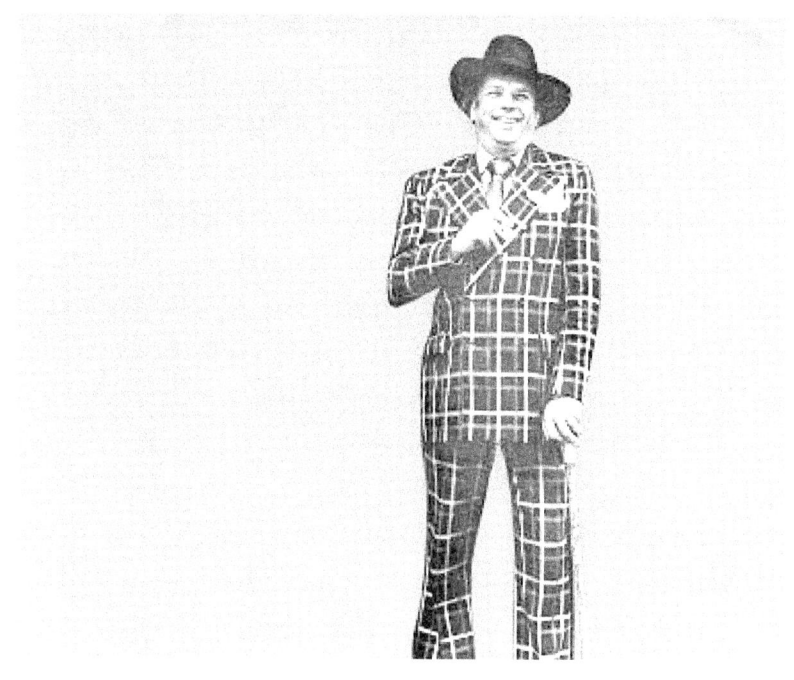

THE MELLY MYTH

A Personal View

"I think it's a substitute, it gives one the illusion of freedom, but in the end I don't think art affects life very much — I think it reflects it."

The excellence of all of the great figures I admire, especially those deceased, is best represented by the work they left behind, be it in film, literature or music. That said, the work of every genius, icon or legend is always enhanced by their myth. All of these people create their own myth, whether purposely or not, often through their work but occasionally through their enigma and the documentation of their own lives. Pablo Picasso is a prime example of one such genius who has his own folk lore surrounding him, only his was created through his ever changing art, the revolving door of lovers and friends, and the sheer size of his persona. Salvador Dali was another example, a genius crossing too far over into madness, but one very aware of his own fame, power, abilities and charisma, however forced and contrived each was. In the film world, Orson Welles is a man who fits the bill perfectly, a behemoth of immeasurable influence and his very own mythical tale, his told through monumental film work and his status as a walking monument of legend.

For me, George Melly is another such man, though many people might frown or be puzzled why I would line Melly up with the afore mentioned names. But I feel Melly lived a great and varied life, at once nihilistic but also very controlled and considered, so that he didn't miss a minute of his time on this earth, even when drinking until he vomited or raved till he dropped. Melly also created his own mythical world, a strange aura that seemed to circle him when he was alive and has been left behind for anyone interested enough to explore it since, a semi self conscious documentation of a life well lived. He may be a lesser figure than Picasso and legends of that size, but for me Melly is just as important, though that is admittedly a personal view point.

As I write what is basically the epilogue on this book about a long time hero of mine, I am also in the midst of researching and compiling material for a Surrealistic documentary on Melly's life and work. While it delves into his personal world here and there, my main concern is his love and devotion to Surrealism, not as an art movement but as a way of life. The ordinary was extraordinary in

Melly's world, and that much is evident in his graphic and very observational style of writing. Clearly, Melly could see the magic and ironic hilarity in almost every situation, especially in his own, often plain bonkers everyday life.

Writing about Melly is fun and easy, because his life and work were so fascinating to me. However, writing about his legacy is a different thing all together, and more of a challenge, because it depends on ones' idea of the word itself. Not only that, but it also depends on what area of Melly's life and work you are focusing on.

As a jazz man, he remains one of the most loved, fondly remembered and cherished in the history of British music, charisma personified in the purest sense. Often out of it on stage, the more lewd and bolshie he got the more the fans loved it. Yet despite his drinking and bawdy antics on the stage, he remained a figure of almost respectable composure, gloriously English even when unconscious under the piano.

As a writer, I challenge anyone to name a better memoirist than he, given the wide range of topics and adventures that feature within his books. You want tales of hedonism and sexual escapades in the navy? You got it; go to Rum, Bum and Concertina. You want reflections of old age? Then read Slowing Down. You want to know what the British Trad Jazz revival was like? OK, then read Owning Up. Through his memoirs is told the unlikely life of an upper middle class scouser who could mix with everyone, with every background, colour or creed. It's that cross over appeal again which is hard to explain and impossible to define. His books can be smutty and hugely intelligent at the same time, and they often are. Contradictory certainly, but also ridiculously engaging.

Then there's the Surrealism. In many ways he is the ultimate Surrealist. He did not see it merely as a way of expressing oneself through Dali-esque art, but as a tool, a way of viewing life, or at least of seeing the world; awareness, consciousness, unconsciousness, the absurd, the ordinary, the extraordinary, the uncanny, and the certainty of chance, the latter being his motto in life.

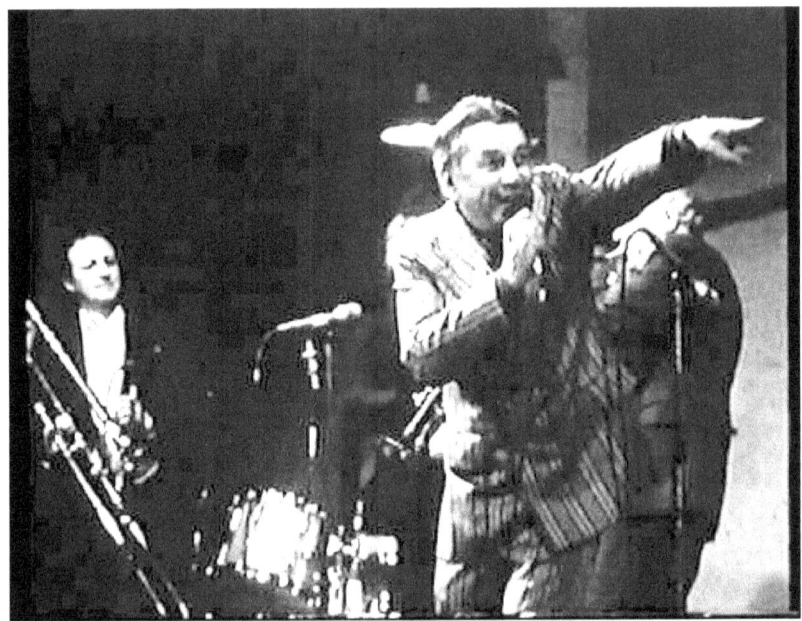

To many people, George summed up perfectly the idea of care free bohemia, of eccentricity, the idea of being larger than life and loving every minute of it. Melly though, did not see himself as a bohemian in any way. "As an old Surrealist," he said and quite rightly too, "I have always mistrusted bohemianism as such. Bohemianism is simply the licence for eccentricism. You know, someone with a big hat, with illegitimate children... People like Bunuel (Luis Bunuel, Surrealist filmmaker) are not at all bohemian, they are Surrealist;

156

very correct in their clothes and behaviour and deportment except when they wish to create scandal. They were not the wide-hatted, bearded, drunken, wenching prototype image of a bohemian. But in fact bohemianism is basically a middle class thing."

In my view Melly is not getting the credit he deserves in any area, for too few younger people are even aware of his work. This is a shame, for even just a push in the right direction - if interested in jazz, Surrealism or the undeniable lure of myth - could lead them into a new area of understanding. But at the end of the day, whether George Melly is remembered for the next few decades seems irrelevant, for the man himself, though vein when it came to fame and his towering ego, probably couldn't care less how he was being perceived after his death. And as a firm atheist and humanist, could Melly really be looking down from some mighty, heavenly place, a grinning angel with wings hovering over the earth, his fans, his family, his friends and those he loved? Even if heaven does exist, surely Melly the non believer would be too stubborn to come out from his holy quarters to show us that he was wrong for all those years, and that God is actually a pretty nice bloke. For George, what mattered was life itself, and how he chose to live it, consistently, with passion and curiosity.

"You know," George said in 1997, a whole decade before his death. "I started life with an adolescent enthusiasm for three things - Surrealism, Bessie Smith and fly-fishing - and I finish up with exactly the same three. Isn't that extraordinary?"

References and Acknowledgements

Thanks to Diana Melly, Elda Abramson, Tom Melly, Louisa Buck, Paul Willets, Wally Fawkes, Susan Fawkes, Adam Smith, and Digby Fairweather.

Articles referred to;
Sabotage Times
Book and Magazine Collector
The Guardian
The Independent
Standard
The Observer archive
Alternatives to Valium
New York Times
Strangled Magazine
Dancing Ledge...
Melody Maker
Susan De Muth Melly interview
The Times
Roger Ebert's Website

Footage and audio;
George Melly: The Journey, Arena, 1978
Surreal Thing, Imagine, Alan Yentob
Outsider Art Documentary
George Melly's Last Stand
BBC Radio Archive

Melly on Parkinson, 1977

Melly on 5's Company, 1997

This is Your Life, 1993

Books;

Diana Melly - Take A Girl Like Me

Diana Melly - Strictly Ballroom

Digby Fairweather - On the Road With George Melly

George Melly - Owning Up

George Melly - Rum, Bum and Concertina

George Melly - Scouse Mouse

George Melly - Paris and the Surrealists

George Melly - Hooked

George Melly - Slowing Down

George Melly - Don't Tell Sybil

George Melly - Revolt Into Style

ABOUT CHRIS WADE

Chris Wade is a UK based writer, artist, filmmaker and musician. As well as running the acclaimed music project Dodson and Fogg, he has written books on The Kinks, Malcolm McDowell, Captain Beefheart, Robert De Niro and many others. He has also released audiobooks of his comedic fiction, such as Cutey and the Sofaguard, narrated by Rik Mayall. His other projects include Rainsmoke, a musical outfit with actor Nigel Planer, and Hound Dawg Magazine, for which he has interviewed such people as Sharon Stone, Donovan and Jethro Tull's Ian Anderson. His art films include The Apple Picker (accepted by Sydney World Film Festival, featuring Toyah Willcox and Nigel Planer), and Cuentos. He also made a documentary about George Melly called George Melly: The Certainty of Hazard.

More info at his website: wisdomtwinsbooks.weebly.com